The Foreigner

DESMOND STEWART

The Foreigner

A SEARCH FOR
THE FIRST-CENTURY JESUS

HAMISH HAMILTON
LONDON

First published in Great Britain 1981
by Hamish Hamilton Ltd
Garden House 57–59 Long Acre London WC2E 9JZ

The publishers are grateful for the permission granted
to the author to quote from the *Jerusalem Bible*
published and © 1966 by Darton, Longman & Todd
Ltd and Doubleday & Co. Inc, from *Jesus* by Michael
Grant published by Weidenfeld & Nicolson, from
The Quest of the Historical Jesus by Albert Schweitzer
published by Adam and Charles Black, and from *Jesus
the Jew* by Geza Vermes published by Collins
Publishers.

British Library Cataloguing in Publication Data

Stewart, Desmond
    The foreigner.
    1. Jesus Christ
    2. Anthroposophy
    I. Title
    232   BT304.97
    ISBN 0–241–10686–9

Printed and bound in Great Britain by
REDWOOD BURN LTD
Trowbridge, Wiltshire

To Alan Neame – In Four Decades of Friendship

Qui mecum sunt, non me intellexerunt

They that are with me have not understood me[1]

[1] Joachim Jeremias regards this (cf. *Unknown Sayings of Jesus*, London, 1964) as one of the uncanonical Sayings with a good claim to being authentic. It is found in the Latin version of the *Apocryphal Acts of Peter*. (*Acta apostolorum apocrypha* I, ed. Lipsius, 1891; reprinted Darmstadt, 1959.)

CONTENTS

Contents

Foreword

Sadly I write this obituary foreword to *The Foreigner*. Desmond
Stewart was my intimate friend for forty years. We were exact contemporaries and met at Oxford when we were both seventeen. As Julian
Evans remarked at his funeral, he had an extraordinary capacity for
changing the course of other people's lives for mental and physical
adventure. Certainly the course of mine was changed that day early in
the war when he came into my rooms at Wadham, wearing his camel-
hair coat (like John the Baptist), and explained how vitally important it
was that I should immediately join the Peace Pledge Union. But that
was only the beginning. Our ways were always diverging and converg-
ing. Had that first meeting not occurred, I should never have spent
years as his colleague in the Middle East, in Iraq where we taught at the
University of Baghdad, in the Lebanon where we were once nearly
murdered by a brigand, in Egypt where we worked as journalists; nor
should I have had that wonderful drive from Baghdad to Paris by way
of Istanbul. I should not have watched this, his last book, growing
through every stage to completion, or be writing these words now.

Desmond had an enormously powerful intellect, fortified by a classical education. His memory was amazingly retentive, and as a writer he
was the complete professional: regular, endlessly energetic, invariably at work by 6 am, fertile, meticulously accurate in research,
lyrical often in expression – poems, novels, plays, articles, portraits of
cities and indeed whole cultures, histories – never without a work on
hand, always enthusiastic over the next to be undertaken. I think he
never had a manuscript refused. I know he never wrote anything
second-rate or dull. He was not as well known in England as he should
have been, but this was because the subject of which he was master, the
culture and politics of the Middle East, was not, unfortunately, one to
catch the imagination of the English world at large. He died at the peak
of his form, having in the last ten years of his life written three magnificently researched and profoundly intuitive biographies, each of an
epochal figure in the history of the Middle East and indeed of the
world: T. E. Lawrence, Theodor Herzl and Jesus Christ.

The first crisis of an illness that was to prove fatal came immediately after he had sent the completed manuscript of *The Foreigner* to his publishers. The moment he was strong enough to put on his glasses, less than six weeks later, he set about correcting the proofs and reconciling minute inconsistencies in his treatment of that veritable mine-field which is the Synoptic Problem! When the second and final crisis occurred a day or two after, the proofs had already been returned; everything was in order. There was nothing more to be done – except the compiling of the index, which he had asked me to do a long time before. Here I should mention, as Desmond would have wished me to, the invaluable help and guidance of the Reverend Canon Roy Porter, Professor of Theology at Exeter University.

So much for his professionalism. What of his character? He never rested. The key-note of his nature was zeal. He was loyal, tenacious, a born fighter. He loved his family, he loved his friends, he loved the poor and the wronged. He loved justice, he loved truth. He loved the past and eagerly embraced the future. He loved writing. He loved travelling, seeing things, doing things, passing on his knowledge, talking, laughing; the good things of life and its austerities; above all, life itself. But of all the passions that impelled or warred in his nature, the fiercest of all was his passion for Jesus. Strange as this may sound, it was the case. From the first day I met him and long before that, until his latest breath, Jesus was never far from his thoughts or indeed from his lips. It was not the passion of a theologian for an ideal, less still the passion of a devotee for a cult-figure; more that of an athlete wrestling with another athlete, Jacob wrestling with the Angel of the Lord. *I will not let thee go, except thou bless me. Tell me thy name . . .* And *The Foreigner* is the monument to this titanic struggle.

'I have seen the sun at midnight,' he said after pulling through from the first crisis of his illness. These enigmatic words puzzled his family and friends. But the diligent reader of *The Foreigner* will recognise them as a quotation from Chapter 20, where Lucius Apuleius describes what it is to pass through the gates of death. An affirmation, in a word, of the soul's immortality.

In a moving tribute to our old friend, Ian Davie wrote: 'I always felt Desmond had about him a quite extraordinary and absolute assurance of what, for want of a better word, we call eternal life. And now he is gone into the world of Light, I feel that Marcion's Stranger can now be his dearest friend.'

No doubt of it.

Brave soul, dear friend, recalled to the Kingdom of the East, fare-well.

Alan Neame

A Personal Prologue

The title of this book may seem ill-chosen. Jesus is part of the domestic and public culture of the west. Events are dated from the year fixed for his birth, even if it is no longer supposed that AD 1 coincides with his nativity. The day on which he was believed to have conquered death is the Lord's – *Domenica, Dimanche, Kyriakê* – in southern Europe, and although in northern Europe that day is named after the Sun, it is still associated with him. Oaths and insults pay him the indirect tribute of vulgar fame; his supposed birthday makes the December cash-registers rejoice. Most lives in the west, and millions elsewhere, end with some commendation to his care.

So present, yes: but alien as when the earliest Christian books, codices buried in jars to escape the first heresy-hounds, call him *allogenês*, 'of another race'. The men who so named him in fourth-century copies of far older texts used a Greek word that leaps from the neat rows of Coptic script. The further we go back the more foreign appears the man who had nowhere to lay his head. Our planet domesticated him only when humanistic Renaissance painters set him in courts or sentimental pre-Raphaelites among roses or the apparatus of a carpenter's bench. The first known drawing of him shows an ass-headed figure on a cross; his first portraits are hieratic and unearthly. No single tradition has had the authority to fix his appearance. His representations range from the majestic humanity of Michelangelo's *Pietà* to the gigantism of the figure enfolding Rio. Each of us forms his own portrait which inevitably owes much to our predecessors' pictures. Hollywood has shown a crucified filmstar with shaved armpits.

My portrait of Jesus was shaped by my life in a manner which I assume is shared with others. My baptism took place amidst the affectionate blur of parents and their friends. Three godparents, the normal quota, escorted me to the font and became theoretically responsible for my religious right-thinking. My godmother, who soon vanished to Barbados and a long prosperous life, contributed nothing to my notion of Jesus but left me a knitted doll which I knew by her maiden name. One godfather, with claims to be the first Alpinist to scale the Brenva face of Mont Blanc, was an Edwardian physicist fond of Greek statues and of my father but sceptical towards nearly everything else. My favourite, my father's brother, was an engineer by temperament and by accident a physician. Insatiably curious, he bought theological books in order to dispute them. For behind the sceptics of the 1920s stood the ghosts of an earnest generation. Three of my great-grandfathers had been ministers of religion. One, ruler of two unfilled churches in County Limerick, lived to telegraph his protest that I should be christened by an Irish surname. Another, long dead, wore the kilt, preached in Gaelic and for his exertions during a Highland famine received a silver plate, still in my possession. His son, my grandfather, brought Jordan water for the successive baptisms of my sceptical uncle and my reticent father.

Like others born between the Wars I owned a bible illustrating Palestine in the colours of Beatrix Potter. School made the central figure grimmer: guarantor of guilt and, if one was gullible, patron of empire. The bishop who confirmed me was said to have advocated the persecution of conscientious objectors when a young cleric in Bloemfontein: but that town has strange progeny (including the creator of the Hobbit) and may bear the blame. My school had contributed innumerable officers to colonial wars. Dull sermons turned my wandering attention to gilt verses on marble. One linked such heroes to Jesus:

These were his servants. In his steps they trod,
Following through death the martyred Son of God.

Ashanti ... Hong Kong ... Pietermaritzburg: I cannot remember where.

In flight from the Friend of the Bunny Rabbits fused with the Master of the Maxim Gun, I succumbed, at Oxford, to medieval nostalgia. The high altar at Pusey House (I remember a bedlike structure with barley-sugar posts) raised Jesus to an Olympian remoteness. At that time I had not learnt that the Tractarian in whose honour the house was named had advocated clitorectomy for English maidens suspected of a secret sin.

My departure for the middle east was activated in large measure by a desire to escape Oxonian complexities which would sound quaint to a modern reader. Initially I felt no attraction to Islam. I had inherited the medieval condemnation of that religion for what has been diagnosed as its inherent violence and for its refusal to allow rational disputation. I was agreeably surprised to discover that my Iraqi students detested the thought of war and were open to the discussion of most ideas. The puzzles of Oxford, the symptoms of a faith wished for rather than attained, were replaced in Baghdad and Cairo by a general sense that under the human trapeze hung a providential net. Unlike his western counterpart, an Arab Marxist would think it eccentric to plan a secular interment. For the middle east saw God as the neckvein's neighbour, whether the neck belonged to a prince or bootblack. The mosque belonged to the earthy and normal, not to the congenitally religious or the slightly mad. Jesus was honoured as no more than a major prophet: but to say 'no more than' must convey the reverence for the holy which the Muslims have retained as a daily tincture. At the same time such a religious society shows the fluidity of fact. The recent past becomes part of mythology, the immediate future part of apocalypse. A Baghdad jockey, calling round to offer tips for tomorrow's racing, could suddenly start affirming that the proliferation of short-sleeved women proclaimed that the door of repentance was about to slam and we'd all be for it.

In adopting Jesus as its god Europe has often overlooked his Jewish origins. But his links with a Hellenised Levant, where ideas and fashions were exchanged between neighbours and antagonists, were ignored even more. Everyone now recognises the lethal absurdity of the nineteenth-century German study, *Was Christ an Aryan?*[1] But to picture the Jews of the first century as like their descendants today, or to imagine that Jesus may be assimilated to any twentieth-century western model, is no less misleading.

The life of Jesus as purveyed in western churches, cinemas and theatres, thence filtering down to the generality, incorporates, throughout the many versions, certain common features. The following gives a rough approximation:

In a Galilee with no particular affinities a virgin, still only affianced to her husband, becomes pregnant. Joseph, this future husband, a carpenter from Nazareth, knows that he at any rate is not the father. An angel intervenes to explain the baby's destiny and name. In a manner recalling the Scots adage, 'Every Stewart thinks himself kith to the king,' Joseph claims lineal descent from the eleventh-century David. This lineage obliges him to travel to the township of David's father and Mary is delivered of her firstborn son in Bethlehem. Associated in western fancy with the snows of winter, the town just south of Jerusalem was expected to produce the messiah, a national liberator, variously interpreted by the few Old Testament prophets who described him. Two variants of the infancy of Jesus are current. In one, duly presented at the Temple, he is taken home to Nazareth by his parents; in another, a dream counsels Joseph to take the child and his mother to Egypt, since Herod is planning a massacre of boy-children in the Bethlehem region. However, Jesus is imagined as brought up in Galilee. The household contains brothers and sisters, half-brothers and half-sisters, or, in a common Catholic rendering of the Greek *adelphoi*, cousins. Jesus is thought to divide his youth between his father's work-

[1] Cf. A. Muller: *Jesus ein Arier*, Leipzig, 1904.

bench and religious studies. The latter make him an infant prodigy. Aged twelve, he confutes men learned in the Jewish law. His studies also make him strictly Jewish (in the emphasis of one gospel) but, in the eyes of Jewish experts at the time, a disregarder of basic Jewish rules. This puzzle is solved by the argument that Jesus stresses the inner, spiritual nature of the law. In any event, aged about thirty, and during the fifteenth year of Tiberius as Caesar, Jesus, a bachelor, inter-rupts a routine of provincial living. After accepting baptism at the hands of a Judaean holy man, he starts healing the sick, preaching repentance, recruiting disciples and predicting a new order. His mission is largely confined to the north-west shores of Lake Galilee, whose chief city, Tiberias, Jesus avoids. Instead, he preaches in the synagogue at Capernaum, a stone's throw from the substantial house of a future disciple, Simon Peter, and his wife. Jesus attracts at least one female penitent from the large lakeside town of Magdala, a few miles south of Capernaum.

The mission reveals Jesus, in standard belief, as the Messiah, even though he is very unlike the popular conception of that national libera-tor. His success as a healer (except in upland Nazareth, where his powers desert him) has impressed a rural society without hospitals for the curing or concealing of the sick. But although attracting many, he fails to win a serious following. His message that God is about to install a new order seems unconfirmed; fishermen are incapable of meeting the sharpness of his Jewish opponents, prompted, in the traditional view, by malice or the devil.

The background to the mission is pictured in one of two ways. Those whose imagination draws on Renaissance, pre-Raphaelite or Symbolist paintings imagine vistas of marble and mosaic. Those aware of archaeological research know that Capernaum was a lakeside hamlet, built of lugubrious black basalt from the Golan hills. The heaviness of bleak volcanic walls supports light wooden roofs which can be opened to permit an invalid's stretcher to be lowered within. The synagogue where Jesus taught was the modest forerunner of the stately pillared building built later and now reconstructed. Whatever its townscapes, Galilee retains a hilly beauty marked by a sense of remoteness from the world.

The comparative failure of his mission persuades Jesus (who has de-livered himself of paradoxical sermons and parables) to go to Jerusa-lem. He knows this will lead to a clash with authority. Accompanied by twelve disciples – the number echoes that of the ancient tribes – he follows the Jordan valley to stay briefly at Bethany before entering the holy city for his final week. At a last supper he institutes two sacra-ments. A disciple who has betrayed him for thirty pieces of silver helps his foes to arrest him. Abashed, in the traditional view, by the superior virtues of his teaching and practice, the priestly authorities contrive his execution. The season is early spring and the occasion is Passover. Crucified between two bandits after a parody of justice, he dies in three hours and is buried shortly before sunset by secret adherents from the ruling class. On the third day, in claimed accord with an Old Testament text, he rises from the dead and on Sunday morning disciples find an empty tomb. An approximate month now follows in which Jesus spasmodically appears to various followers in various places. He seems fully physical (being apprehensible by touch and able to eat fish) but has mysterious properties which enable him to pass through closed doors or conceal his identity even from intimates. He then vanishes into the heavens.

This outline – or something like it – has served as intellectual support for very contrasted ways of looking at the career and significance of Jesus. In traditional orthodoxy, he is the pivot of a system of global salvation. In evangelical sects he prompts the personal experience of redemption. In the minds of less theological admirers he seems the preacher of an ethical system uniquely humane.

My wish to discover what literal truth lies behind the theological or humanistic interpretations was sharpened by my experience, in the 1970s, of writing biographies. In the first, my life of Theodor Herzl, the founder of political Zionism, I had probed a character on whom his followers had forced, not with his entire consent, a messianic role in the modern mode. T. E. Lawrence had also been seen in messianic terms by himself and a variety of admirers. In the study of both men I became aware how the isolation of specific, undeniable truths can modify the structure round which the portrait has formed. Herzl has served as model for Moses in at least one stained glass window; yet to the anti-Semites of a neurotic Europe he loomed as the monstrous contriver of a world conspiracy. The Herzl of reality, it was not hard to discover, was neither the pious Jew of the synagogue window nor a cruel human being. He never bothered to have his son, Hans, circumcised and in his home circle he disregarded, to the consternation of observant Jews, the food restrictions of the Mosaic code. While accepting the logic of imperialism, along with the British Liberal Party which under Gladstone sanctioned the occupation of Egypt, he would have held aloof from the ruthless methods of contemporary expansionists. But these discoveries were general. My pivotal discovery was the significance of a letter which the twenty-year-old Herzl had written to his friend Heinrich Kana on 8 June, 1880. This letter isolated the effective cause for the failure of his marriage, the deterioration of his wife's health and her early death, and his own desperate dedication to a public life of political action. The letter proved that Herzl had paid the price for assimilating himself to the raffish society of Vienna, contract-

ing the same disease that blighted the life and marriage of the heir to
the Austro-Hungarian throne and culminated in the double suicide at
Mayerling. The same disease almost certainly contributed to Herzl's
early death aged forty-four.

The picture of Lawrence as a pro-Arab guerilla who dedicated his
heart and genius to the liberation of a race could be similarly disproved
with comparative ease. Previous writers had established that the
motives behind his career were those of a British intelligence officer,
not a Che Guevara. But the key to the motivation of Lawrence, particularly during the post-war phase of his existence, was turned by the confessions of a young Scot whom the world-famous colonel, then airman,
employed as partner in a sado-masochistic ritual. These confessions[1]
enabled me to suggest, what few have since denied, that the famous description of the ordeal at Deraa, implicating an Ottoman official, was a
literary invention concealing his entirely voluntary subjection to a
handsome Arab.

The reader must not suppose that the aim of biographers in general,
or this biographer in particular, is to denigrate or destroy. The true biographer believes that what actually happened is more interesting than
fantasy or myth. To one inspired by the search for truth demotion and
promotion are as one. A congenital visionary may emerge deflated but
a misrepresented monarch may, like Richard III, emerge enhanced. It
is no longer possible to believe that Lawrence was the kind of figure he
projected to the young Robert Graves or the trusting Liddell Hart.
The achievement that remains is of a more internal, even spinsterly
kind. The once fancied ability to pass as an Arab and create new kingdoms must yield to the ability to impress such contrasted admirers as
George Bernard Shaw, Winston Churchill and John Bruce, who
arranged his flagellatory antics. Herzl, on the other hand, gained when
salvaged from the propagandists. The man behind *The State for the
Jews* or *Old-New-Land* was more complex, more interesting than the
tract or the utopian novel would suggest.

When I started on my search for the first-century Jesus I knew that it
would be insane to expect such documents as Herzl's letter to Kana or
Bruce's memoir of a master-slave relationship. There would be
nothing to set against Herzl's immense, self-revealing *Diaries* or
Lawrence's equally self-revealing *Seven Pillars of Wisdom*. All Jesus
would share with these two lesser figures were the palings of propaganda around his existence. I would find equivalents to the adulatory

[1] First published by Phillip Knightley and Colin Simpson in *The Sunday Times* and
then in *The Secret Lives of Lawrence of Arabia*, London, 1969.

works on Lawrence which appeared in the 1920s and 1930s and, in Herzl's case, to the hagiographic entries which pack the many volumes of the Herzl Year Book. To get behind palings nineteen hundred years old I should have to use different techniques.

The Jesus who has emerged as 'the foreigner' seems to me – and I can speak for no one else – more coherent and more plausible than the saviour, blood-victim or humane legislator of popular myth. Fitting neither Galilean meadows nor the altars of sacrificial atonement, he seems to me close to the gnostic vision of the essential alien. What the gnostics recognised as foreign was his very nature in the world they knew. Bisecting the material cosmos, not continuing it in a messianic direction, Jesus, or Chrestus, was foreign to the furniture, physical and mental, of the Greco-Roman world; to the attitudes and obsessions of his time; to the country in which he acted, spoke and died; to the religious values of the society which claimed his allegiance. For so apprehending his nature – not for their often grotesque cosmogonies – the gnostics deserve the respect which is returning to them fifteen centuries after they were hounded into silence. Since the role which this first-century Jesus found important was that of one imparting a liberating knowledge, he may seem closer to a yogi than a Christian clergyman: in the sense that London is nearer to Moscow than it is to Pnom Penh. If so it seems, so be it.

D. S.
Tiberias, AD 1981.

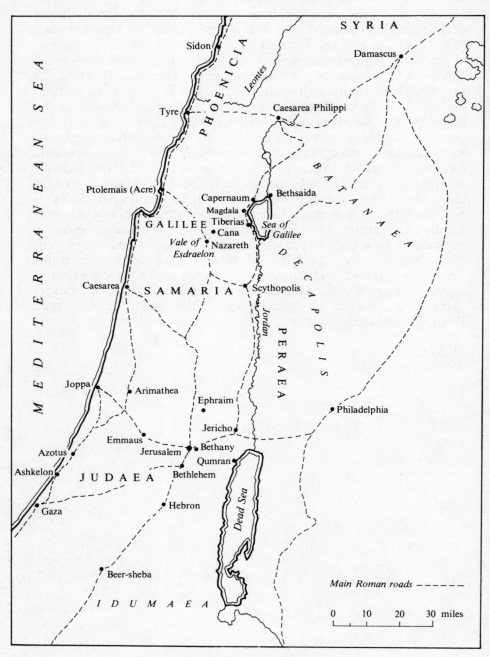

Palestine in the time of Jesus

Part One

JOURNEY TO A SUMMER PASSION

CHAPTER ONE

An Irregular Birth

Jesus was, like other men, born in a particular place and time. This is true whether we consider him, as members of his family did on one occasion, a maniac, a heretic, as he seemed to conventional Jews, a god incarnate, as the Church has taught since it defined its creeds in the third century, a wonder-worker, as he seemed to his first public, or an ethical pioneer. But since he did not belong to the Roman empire's ruling elite and attracted attention only towards the close of a short life, we can name neither the year nor place of his birth with any certainty.

The middle east, where he undoubtedly lived and died, has an aptitude for the imprecise. The first biographies of the twentieth-century Egyptian, Gamal Abdul Nasser, disagreed as to whether he had been born in a village near Assiout, or in the Bacos quarter of Alexandria. Questions of ideology were involved: some wished to portray the supplanter of King Farouk as a peasant while others as a Mediterranean statesman.[1] If this could be the case with the second Egyptian president, how much more easily has it been the case with a man born almost two thousand years ago destined to be the centre of tornados of debate.

Of the four accounts of aspects of his life which open the New Testament, and which for all their limitations form the richest primary source, two tell us nothing about their hero's birth. Mark introduces the adult Jesus, nine verses into his gospel, walking to the Jordan while John's haunting prologue discourses on a pre-cosmic event but ignores any reference to physical nativity.

The gospels of Matthew and Luke, which do speak of his birth, read as though written by those who had never seen Jesus in the flesh but who attempt, each in his own way, to glorify his history.[2]

---

[1] In 1962 this author was writing a book about the Arab world for a New York publisher and needed to know for certain. As he boarded his flight, a functionary from the information department handed him a handwritten note from the minister responsible: 'The President prefers to have been born in Alexandria.'

[2] For the author's approach to the gospels as sources, the reader is referred to Appendix A.

Their accounts of his birth unlock a curiosity-shop of details which are sometimes so picturesque as to clamour for fairy tale depiction or, as with their genealogies, so flat as to make the reader hasten ahead. Nor do they agree, even on Jesus's pedigree. The wonders and enormities surrounding Matthew's account of the birth, the romantic tales and domestic relationships in Luke, force us to ask, with some scepticism, which, if any, of the events may conceal a fact.

The events begin, for Luke, not with the birth of Jesus himself but with that of his cousin and forerunner, John. The elderly priest Zacharias, serving his turn in the temple sanctuary, is ministering at the altar of incense when the angel Gabriel appears to announce that his long barren wife, Elizabeth, is to give birth to a son destined to play the role of Elijah. (In popular belief Elijah was to be the precursor of the mysterious yet mortal messiah.) For his incredulity Zacharias is struck dumb. Six months later Gabriel is despatched on a second errand, this time to a young girl, Mary, betrothed but not yet married to one Joseph, of the house of David. The pair live in Galilee, the hilly inland district to the north of Samaria. Mary, who has never had sexual relations with a man, is told that she is going to have a baby; she is also told of the pregnancy of her elderly cousin Elizabeth. In haste she travels south to the Judaean village, unnamed, where Elizabeth lives. Three signs presage the destiny of the child she carries. Elizabeth's foetus leaps in the womb; the holy spirit guides Elizabeth to recognise Mary's son for what he is to be; Mary intones a hymn – the Magnificat – largely composed from Old Testament quotations. Mary stays long enough for Elizabeth to be delivered and her son circumcised. John's birth releases his father's tongue in a predictive hymn. His son will be the prophet of a long-foretold national liberator; the boy will go before someone evidently divine, yet distinct from the Most High, since the Most High is 'to bring the rising Sun to visit us'.

After a sentence devoted to John's spiritual and physical growth and desert residence Luke falls silent about him for the next three decades.

Having introduced, in a minor key, the theme of birth, Luke introduces a new statement of fact:

> Caesar Augustus issued a decree for a census of the whole world to be taken. This census – the first – took place while Quirinius was governor of Syria, and everyone went to his own town to be registered. So Joseph set out from the town of Nazareth in Galilee and travelled up to Judaea, to the town of David called Bethlehem, since he was of David's house and line, in order to be registered together with Mary, his betrothed, who was with child.[1]

[1] Luke 2, 1–5: the *Jerusalem Bible* (hereafter referred to as JB). Other sources of bibli-

This census has been dated to AD 6, when Herod's son Archelaus had been replaced by a Roman governor. Although Herod the Great and Archelaus had been only nominally independent, Augustus would have been too tactful to command a census in their kingdom during their reigns. Mary gives birth to Jesus and because of the fullness of the inn, lays him in a manger. Angels meanwhile appear to shepherds living in the nearby fields. They announce, not the Most High himself, nor the rising Sun, but 'Christ the Lord'. On the eighth day the baby is circumcised and named Jesus as the Angel had instructed. At a ceremony for Mary's purification (since childbirth made a woman ritually unclean) an old sage, Simeon, salutes the child as

a light to lighten the pagans and the glory of your people Israel.

Simeon predicts that Jesus will cause the fall and rising of many in Israel, that he will be a sign which will be rejected and that Mary's heart will be pierced by a sword

so that the secret thoughts of many will be laid bare.[1]

An old prophetess Anna again draws attention to the child in a messianic context. The family then go home to Galilee.

The Greek obsession with symmetry (which inspires the three salutations to the unborn Jesus, which balances Elizabeth's miracle with Mary's and Simeon with Anna) is as lacking from Matthew as the Greek feeling for domestic incident. After baldly listing the generations between Abraham and Jesus, Matthew concerns himself more closely than Luke with the story of the virgin birth.

His mother Mary was betrothed to Joseph; but before they came to live together she was found to be with child through the Holy Spirit. Her husband Joseph, being a man of honour and wanting to spare her publicity, decided to divorce her informally.[2]

But in a dream an angel prevents this. The boy, he is told, will save his people from their sins, not, as in Simeon's hymn, from foreign oppressors. Matthew ignores the birth of the Baptist, the Roman census or the journey from Galilee. Jesus is simply born at Bethlehem. Matthew's contribution to the story, or folklore, is a sequence of events set in motion by the arrival in Jerusalem of some wise orientals, their number unspecified. They had seen Jesus's star 'in the east', or (a

---

cal translation are the Authorised Version and Desmond Stewart (DS). All Old Testament quotations are from the former, unless otherwise indicated.
[1] Luke 2, 32 & 35: JB (except that JB has 'may be laid bare').
[2] Matthew 1, 18–19: JB.

preferable translation since these eastern observers of the heavens were by definition situated east of Palestine) 'at its rising' – an astrological, horoscopical and regal event. Herod is told of their presence in his capital and he charges them to report when they find the infant king of the Jews, as the visitors have imprudently entitled the object of their search. The star moves to indicate a particular house. Inside they discover the child with his mother and, after offering presents of gold, frankincense and myrrh, they return to the east by a different route, disobeying Herod. The frustrated king sets in hand a massacre of all boy children under two in the Bethlehem region. But Joseph is forewarned in another dream and leaves by night for Egypt. He stays there until Herod is safely dead. But when he returns, thinking to live in Bethlehem, he finds that Herod has been succeeded as ruler of Judaea by his son Archelaus and so moves north to Nazareth in Galilee, that district being ruled by another of Herod's sons, Herod Antipas.

Matthew's dating, which has Herod the Great (who reigned from BC 40 to 4) still in power at the time of the nativity, conflicts with Luke's, linked to the census organised by Quirinius after Archelaus's deposition in AD 7 had put Judaea under direct imperial rule. Matthew, concerned to show that every action in Jesus's career fulfills some Old Testament text or that every predictive passage is fulfilled by Jesus, sets his birth in David's city of Bethlehem, probably without historical evidence. The Massacre of the Innocents is certainly unhistorical. Since Herod, a partly Arab despot, was despised for his whole-hearted acceptance of Greek manners and styles, Jewish tradition would have remembered the atrocity of regional infanticide if it had been more than retro-injected fantasy. A guiding star may work on a Christmas card but could conduct no travellers on real land to a particular house. Other details, whether charming, bizarre or contradictory, illustrate temperament or editorial purpose in these gospel-writers. Luke is interested in the miraculous. He sentimentalises, or at least humanises, human connections. Thus Jesus and John the Baptist are cousins, though later incidents show them as mutual strangers. Luke's shepherds derive distantly from the literary world which invented pastoral poetry. The gift-bearing kings, the moving star, are part of the Levantine folk-myth, almost of the ghetto. Luke's insertion of songs and hymns, as though they are integral texts, echoes the practice of those classical historians who set speeches composed by themselves in the mouths of famous men. Like the Renaissance painters whom his gospel often inspired, Luke thinks in terms of fleshly, visible angels. Matthew, on the other hand, sees the dream as the vehicle of supernatural information, and in this he belongs to a widespread middle eastern tradition. At Giza in Egypt, a tablet set between the paws of the sphinx narrates how a young prince, resting from the hunt, was asked by the Sun God to clear the sand from his encumbered limbs; Jacob dreamed of a ladder between earth and heaven; Joseph's skill at the interpretation of dreams advanced him at Pharaoh's court.

Yet powerful forces prompt the patterns of even the strangest dreams; drug-induced hallucinations conceal some species of reality. Two important facts are suggested by themes in the infancy gospels of Luke and Matthew – facts which the biographer would otherwise have found it difficult to infer.

The Virgin Birth coheres with the Levantine (but not, in this case, the Jewish) world-view of what was possible and glorious. Greek mythology held that gods had often coupled with mortal woman. Bacchus had been fathered by Zeus on Semele, daughter of Cadmus and Harmonia; outstanding men such as Plato and Alexander the Great were believed to have had divine, not mortal fathers. A knowledge of biology that was to remain very limited until the invention of the microscope made such views credible. While the classical world believed that snakes were engendered from corpses and bees from oxen, the *Physiologus*, a text popular in the middle ages, taught that the vulture reproduced itself spontaneously. But the idea of the divine man, or the man divine on one side of the family, is not found in Jewish scripture, which has its own notion of miraculous birth. This involves, not the coupling of gods with mortals, but the pregnancies of women long past the menopause. These legendary women, including the mothers of Isaac and Samson, perhaps propose an unconscious parable of the ancient Jewish stock, capable in every age of producing surprises. Matthew was misled by the Septuagint, the Greek version of the Old Testament on which most of his contemporaries relied for the text of Isaiah, to imagine that the prophet had written that 'the virgin' – in the full sense of the Greek word 'parthenos', a *virgo intacta* – 'will conceive and give birth to a son and they will call him Emmanuel'.[1] From this same word the nineteenth century was to derive *parthenogenesis*, defined by Charles Darwin in 1859 as 'implying that the mature females ... are capable of producing fertile eggs without the concourse of the male'.

Since the discovery that the female contributes actively to the constitution, not merely the passive nourishment, of the foetus, few scientifically-minded people take this doctrine literally. But the appearance of parthenogenesis in Luke and Matthew has important implications for the biographer of Jesus. Had he been Mary's unquestioned child by Joseph, the ecclesiastical organisation for which the gospels were written would have hesitated to publicise a story enabling its enemies to argue, as many did, that Jesus had been a *mamzer*,

---

[1] The *Jerusalem Bible* translates the relevant verse in Isaiah (7,14) as: 'The maiden is with child and will soon give birth to a son whom she will call Immanuel.'

or bastard.[1]

If Joseph, a kindly, tolerant man, discovered that his young bride-to-be was pregnant, and assumed her the victim of seduction, it is easy to picture him covering up the irregularity rather than subjecting it to the rigours of the religious law. It needed no royal massacre or counselling dream to persuade a shrewd, experienced man to remove her from the proximity of those who would note the rounding of her stomach and whisper scandal at the local well.

It is much less easy even to speculate as to who engendered Jesus, or how, and this makes my attempt to picture his appearance hazardous. If Joseph was not his physical father, the genealogies in Matthew and Luke are irrelevant, since both trace the ancestry of his apparent father, while emphasising that Joseph was not the cause of Mary's pregnancy. It is thus impossible to argue that Jesus was a typical Galilean – even if we knew what that was. Whereas, in the case of a later prophet, we know the colour of Muhammad's eyes and skin, there is no contemporary report, or even reliable tradition, of what Jesus looked like. It is true that, in the early third century, Tertullian wrote that Jesus 'in the days of the flesh had an ugly countenance'.[2] But we would be unwise to rely on Tertullian. As a North African ascetic he manifested the early Christian horror of pagan beauty. He had, too, a theological axe to grind: the linking of Jesus with verses in Isaiah which foretell the abjection of one who 'hath no form nor comeliness ... no beauty that we should desire him'.[3] Today, many people's conception of Jesus may ultimately derive from the *Epistle of Lentulus*, reputedly written by a Roman serving in Judaea during the reign of Tiberius. This letter gives Jesus hair the colour of an unripe hazelnut, grey eyes and the general appearance of a Plantagenet prince. Unfortunately the work cannot be traced earlier than the thirteenth century.[4]

Only the Talmud raises the wraith of a father capable of transmitting genes. The cloudiness is inseparable from a work which was evasive when dealing with what, at the time of its collection, was regarded as an enemy religion. Talmud means 'teaching' in Hebrew; both the Palestinian and Babylonian versions were compiled between AD 200, when animosity between church and synagogue was already sharp, and

[1] Mark, the earliest and least worked-over gospel, knows nothing of the virgin birth but uses a curious expression when Jesus first attracts attention. The surprised villagers refer to him as 'the son of Mary'. In the middle east men are normally referred to as sons of their father (Mark 6,3).

[2] *De Carne Christi*, pp. 211–213; quoted in *The Early Christian Fathers*: Cross, p. 142. The precise quotation is: *Nec humanae honestatis corpus fuit.*

[3] *Isaiah* 52, 14; 53, 2–3.

[4] For full text and description, see Montague Rhodes James: *The Apocryphal New Testament*, Oxford, 1924: p. 478.

AD 600 when the church was the established, and persecuting, religion of the Byzantine empire. The 'Teaching' preserves the academic and judicial discussions of generations of Jewish scholars, none of whom had any doctrinal sympathies with the teachings by then ascribed to Jesus. The Talmud's hints that Jesus was sired by a gentile named Pantera have a curious link with a Roman tombstone commemorating an archer from Tyre, Tiberius Julius Abdes Pantera, who died in Germany. The dates on his funerary inscription fit with the time of Jesus's birth.[1] His names are significant. The first two honour the emperor under whom the archer served and the founder of the Caesarean dynasty. The third name, Abdes, is Semitic and may be a shortened form for Abd Shems, or Servant of the Sun. Shems (in Hebrew 'shamash') is the equivalent of the Pharaonic Rê or the Greek Hêlios, a god honoured in most of the Phoenician cities. The fourth name identifies the soldier with a fierce animal. (The Arabic equivalent of Pantera is Fahd, a name held by many Arabs, including one of the sons of the founder of Saudi Arabia.) His names thus mirror the Levant of the first century: compliments to the ruling dynasty; the military's particular cult of the Sun, which found expression in Mithraism, an originally Persian faith; and the name by which he was known to his barrack comrades.

'It is possible, though not likely,' Dr. Morton Smith has concluded, 'that his tombstone from Bingerbrück is our only genuine relic of the Holy Family.'

During his lifetime, Pantera may have had a Lebanese look – or may not, since Lebanon has undergone much immigration in its turbulent history.

Apart from the irregular birth, Matthew provides another nugget of even greater biographical importance: that Joseph took Mary to Egypt. Elsewhere in his gospel Matthew has Jesus act in such a way as to fulfill a prediction (so far as he understands it – an important proviso). Here he twists a text to an action of which he somehow had come to know, for the scriptural justification for Joseph's departure is taken from Hosea:

> I . . . called my son out of Egypt.

The quotation is the second half of a compound sentence:

> When Israel was a child then I loved him, and I called my son out of Egypt.[2]

Hosea's text is not predictive, let alone messianic. The prophet is referring to the historical Exodus. There was no tradition that the future de-

---

[1] Morton Smith: *Jesus the Magician*, New York, 1978: p. 47.
[2] Hosea 11, 1.

liverer would come from Egypt.

Another link between Jesus and Egypt makes the account more than plausible. Names, as we have seen with Pantera, indicate much. Hegesippus, a Jewish Christian of the mid-second century, identifies the Clopas whose 'Mary' is mentioned at the Crucifixion[1] with the brother of Joseph, Mary's husband. Clopas is the Aramaic form of Cleopatros, the male form of the famous Cleopatra.

First-century Jews frequently adopted Greek names, some for reasons of fashion, others to integrate themselves into Hellenistic society, yet others in compliment to powerful pagans. The historian Josephus, for example, adopted the name Flavius out of an admiration for the dynasty of Vespasian, whom he claimed to recognise as a secular messiah. (In the Iraq of the 1920s it was not unknown for Iraqi fathers to name their children after British generals such as Cox or Townsend.) The name of Joseph's brother would easily be explained if he had been born in Egypt. It would also help us to guess his approximate age. Cleopatra started her reign in BC 51 and died nineteen years later. If Clopas had been given his Ptolemaic name in honour of the start of her reign, he would have been around eighty at the time of his nephew's crucifixion. At the other extreme, he is not likely to have been given this name later than BC 44, the year of a major famine. 'Cleopatra opened the royal granaries in Alexandria and distributed corn to the citizens. From this distribution the Jews were excluded – rightly so, by the letter of the law, since they were not citizens of Alexandria, although they lived there.'[2] Alexandria has claims to be the cradle of anti-Semitism. Jews were hated, not for any supposed usurious tendencies, but for their abstention from the pagan rites which were an essential part of citizenship in the Ptolemaic capital. The Jews reciprocated and in general supported the Romans. 'I would have conquered,' Cleopatra supposedly declared, 'if I had been able to destroy all the Jews.'[3]

Therefore, unless his family were strikingly out of sympathy with communal attitudes, Clopas would have been named before the famine of BC 44. A likely year is 47. A year earlier, Julius Caesar (a popular hero of the Jews) had landed in Alexandria. His son by Cleopatra, Caesarion, was born a year later. The occasion signalled a brief moment of ethnic harmony. The half-Greek, half-Roman prince was to be king in name from BC 44 to 30. If Clopas shared the birth-year of Caesarion, he would have been middle-aged at the time of his nephew's birth and old at the time of his execution. Such a time-scheme would

---

[1] John 19, 25. Grammatically, she could be his wife or daughter.
[2] Hans Volkmann: *Cleopatra, A Study in Politics and Propaganda*; tr. T. J. Cadoux, New York, 1958: p. 91.
[3] Ibid, p. 199.

fit with the supposition that Joseph had fathered an earlier family by another wife.

There would have been nothing out of the way if a branch of Jesus's family had been established in Egypt. Alexandria was the world's largest Jewish city and Jews lived in large numbers throughout the delta and the Nile valley. This Jewish presence was symbolised by the existence in the delta of the only Jewish temple (as distinct from synagogue) outside Jerusalem. The ex-High Priest Onias IV had founded it under Ptolemaic patronage at Leontopolis around BC 170. It was to function for one year longer than the temple in Jerusalem itself. Not all Jews felt that they could fulfill their religious obligations in it, since scripture had decreed that Jerusalem alone was valid for regular sacrifice. And economics rather than religion had drawn Jews in such numbers to the kingdom of the Ptolemies. Living in Egypt, they depended on Palestine for olive oil. Clopas and his family may well have imported this commodity from Galilee. Such oil was a major export to the diaspora in Syria, Babylonia, Kurdistan and Anatolia, as well as in Egypt.

CHAPTER TWO

Out of Egypt

In taking seriously Matthew's mention of the flight into Egypt I am at odds, I must warn the reader, with those many commentators who take the flight to be a *midrash* (or homiletic expansion) on such ancient stories as the sale of Joseph into Egypt or the abduction of Jeremiah. I am not swayed by the applicability of Matthew's text from Hosea but rather by points of consistence with what happens later.

Matthew's contribution is limited to the stark fact that the family left Palestine. For their route and destination, local traditions and apocryphal tales need to be balanced against common sense.[1]

According to an Armenian infancy gospel, which cannot be proved to antedate the twelfth century, Joseph took Mary on a somewhat zigzag course. After following the coastal plain to Ashkelon, they doubled inland to ancient Hebron and only thereafter struck west again for the main coastal highway through Gaza, Khan Yunis and Rafah. If we rule out any particular dread of Herod, the somewhat indirect nature of the itinerary could be explained by Joseph's need to attend to business or buy things for the journey. From the modern Al-Arish[2] the highway followed the Mediterranean shore to Pelusium. This now vanished metropolis once dominated north-west Sinai but the customs post for Egypt was at Kantara, a bridge over lake and marsh into the delta. What such a frontier town was like we can see from Dimi on the opposite, Libyan edge of the delta. Its ruins are accessible to those who sail across Lake Karoun and mount the sandy desert to where an impressive causeway still leads into what was a settlement for soldiers and officials. A sloppily built pharaonic temple honoured the ruler, whether a Ptolemy or a Caesar, under the aspect of an Egyptian god. A treasury had a safe room with a beehive roof for storing taxes.

The travellers' obvious route will have been west along the Wadi Tumulat, a traditional point of entry for visitors or invaders from the east. Leaving the delta's eastern province by crossing the Damietta

[1] Cf. Otto F. A. Meinardus: *Christian Egypt, Ancient and Modern*, Cairo, 1965.
[2] A report that criminals were sent there to have their noses bobbed may explain its Greek name, Rhinocolura, or derive as a legend from it.

branch of the Nile at Sammanud (here Coptic tradition, Armenian gospel and common sense agree), they traversed the western province to reach the branch of the Nile which flowed into the sea at Canopus, a resort town linked to Alexandria by a thronged canal. At the point where they crossed they could see Wadi Natrun, the later centre of monasticism, shimmering as a scaly white depression to the west.

Their itinerary so far suggests that their goal was Alexandria. Yet church tradition has them moving abruptly south for the ancient On, the centre of the Egyptian sun cult and close to the modern Heliopolis.[1] The traditional itinerary seems logical as far as Kantara and probable to the western branch of the Nile. Its obvious conclusion would have been a short boat trip to Alexandria. However, prudential reasons worked to exclude Alexandria from accounts of Jesus's childhood. Throughout much of their history the Romans had a foreboding that power would pass from Italy. Their annihilation of Carthage, and the unchivalrous rejoicing by so civilised a poet as Horace when Cleopatra killed herself, are explained by this fear. Christianity would have been that much more unpopular if it had been associated too intimately with Alexandria. An Alexandrian claim to the boyhood and intellectual formation of Jesus would have completely overshadowed Rome's claim to the tombs of Simon Peter and Paul.

Joseph probably began his journey a few weeks after Mary's pregnancy was established beyond doubt but before it could attract public notice. The pair will have entered Egypt as the itineraries suggest. They would then have struck west across the delta, intending to sail down the Canopic branch of the Nile to Alexandria; but travel in the middle east has always been subject to delays. Mary's pregnancy probably reached an advanced stage when they were still somewhere in the heavily populated central delta. This could explain the otherwise inexplicable reverse of direction towards the south. A church at Mattariya (in what is now northern Cairo) preserves a stone trough, incised with hieroglyphs, in which Mary is reputed to have washed her infant's clothes. The connection with the flight goes back to the middle ages at least. Emmanuel Piloti, a Venetian merchant of Cretan origin, wrote, in the early fifteenth century, of a garden three miles from Cairo on the Jerusalem road, 'where is a well, worked in white marble, which seems as though it had been made today. It is full of sweet water in which Our Lady washed the clothes of Our Lord Jesus Christ.'

After the birth and the conclusion of Joseph's business calls in Old Cairo (formerly Babylon), the holy family probably travelled downstream by felucca or similar craft to Leontopolis (now Tell al-

[1] The Coptic tradition that the holy family travelled far south up-river is probably a pious invention to dignify such cities as Assiout (dedicated to the wolf-god) by association with the supplanters of Isis and Horus.

Yahudiya, or Hill of Jewry); it was most likely here, at the only Temple proper outside Palestine, that the child was presented. To reach Alexandria, they would then have struck west at Sammanud to reach the Canopic branch of the Nile and take another felucca to the coast.

If Jesus was born in Egypt, not Palestine, near Heliopolis, not Bethlehem, it explains much of the symbolism which attracted him later in life. For more than three thousand years Heliopolis had been the centre of the solar cult. A distinctive symbol stood for the sun's power; a myth conveyed a vision of the relationship between the eternal and the transient. The symbol was the obelisk, a tapering stone shaft with a pyramidal tip, still used as the indicator of the giant sunclocks formed by several Roman piazze. The myth concerns the phoenix. Herodotus, writing in the middle of the fifth century BC, preserves the first western account. The Greek inquirer learned that the phoenix was a bird which arrived in Heliopolis every five centuries from the east, bearing its father, embalmed in a globe of Arabian myrrh, whom it then buried in the temple of the sun. Herodotus was shown representations of a bird 'with golden and red plumage'. Pliny the naturalist, born towards the end of Jesus's life, reports that there is never more than one phoenix alive at any one time. At the close of a long life it weaves itself a nest of cassia twigs and frankincense. A worm destined to become its successor then grows from the old bird's carcass. Tacitus, writing in the century after Jesus, records that the phoenix had been seen in the reigns of Sesostris, Amasis II and Ptolemy III. The most developed account occurs in the same medieval bestiary that postulated the self-generation of vultures. The *Physiologus* describes the phoenix as an Indian bird which, after subsisting on air for five centuries, loads its wings with unguents, flies to the sun temple and is burned to ashes. 'Next day the young phoenix is already feathered; on the third day its pinions are grown; it salutes the sun priests and flies away.'

Myths have the useful function of expanding the bonds of imagination. No one who had lived near Heliopolis, no woman whose child was born there, could fail to attach importance to the legend of the phoenix or to ponder its implications. Two points are worth remarking in a legend which has more points of contact with the Jesus of history than the fable of a military redeemer, or messiah. First the gold, frankincense and myrrh which the sages traditionally offered the child have echoes in the Heliopolitan myth. Second the Greek word *phoenix*, and its pharaonic equivalent, *benu*, both have the secondary meaning of date-palm. There is an echo of this connection in the Koranic story[1]

[1] *Koran XIX, 23: And the pangs of labour drove her to the bole of a palm-tree. 'Would that I had died before this,' she said. 'Would that I had been forgotten and out of mind!'*

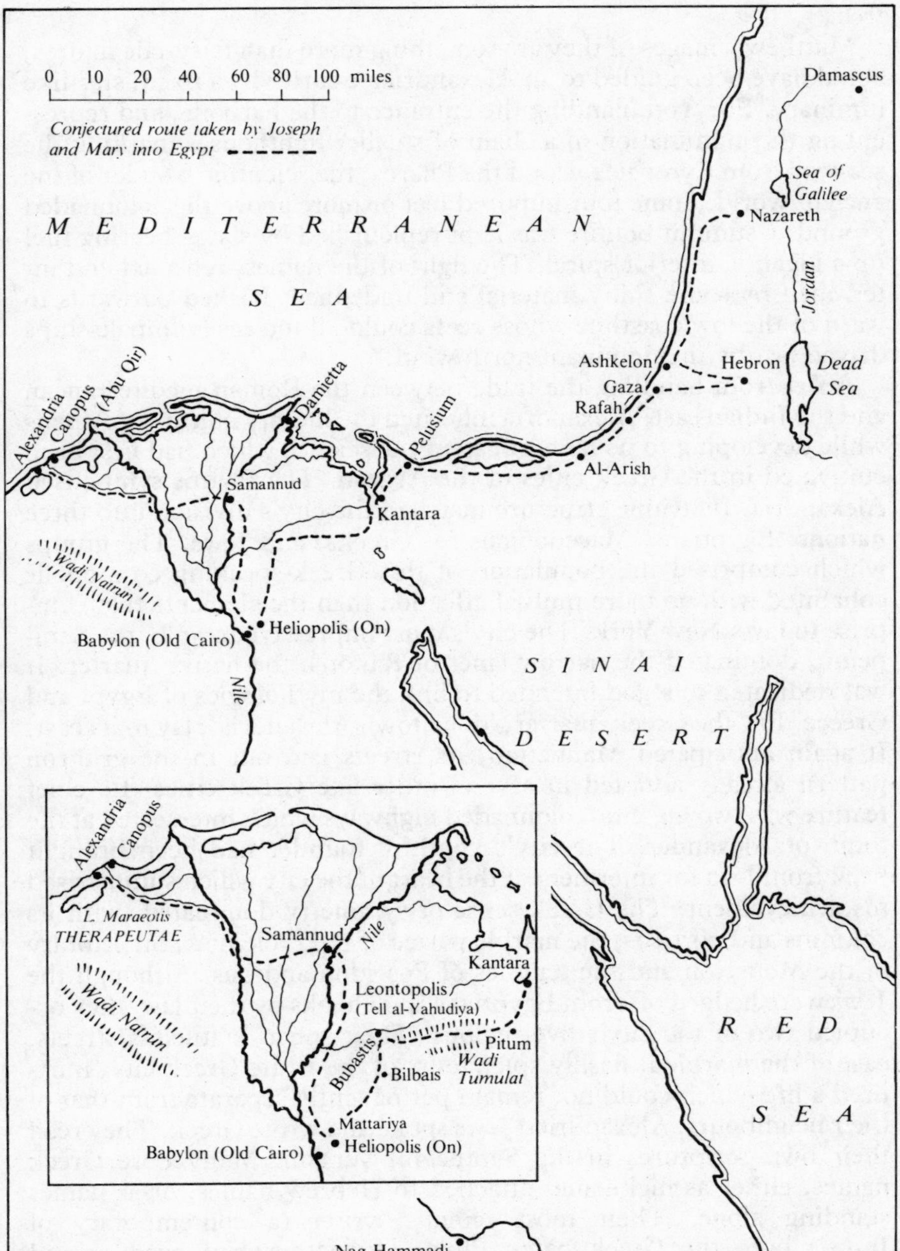
0 10 20 40 60 80 100 miles
Conjectured route taken by Joseph and Mary into Egypt
Damascus
Sea of Galilee
Nazareth
Jordan
MEDITERRANEAN SEA
Ashkelon
Hebron
Dead Sea
Gaza
Rafah
Al-Arish
Alexandria
Canopus
(Abu Qir)
Damietta
Pelusium
Samannud
Kantara
Wadi Natrun
Heliopolis (On)
Babylon (Old Cairo)
Nile
SINAI DESERT
Alexandria
Canopus
L. Maraeotis
THERAPEUTAE
Samannud
Nile
Kantara
Wadi Natrun
Leontopolis
(Tell al-Yahudiya)
Bubastis
Pitum
Wadi Tumulat
Bilbais
Mattariya
Babylon (Old Cairo)
Heliopolis (On)
RED SEA
Nag Hammadi

The road to Egypt

that Jesus was born, not in a Bethlehem cattle-shed, but under a palm-tree.

Matthew's mages, if they are something more than fairy-tale figures, could have been guided to an Alexandrian quarter by a fixed, star-like luminary. For, commanding the entrance to the harbour, and representing the culmination of a chain of smaller lighthouses marking the sea-way from Cyrenaica, stood the Pharos, the scientific wonder of the ancient world. Some four hundred feet or more above the colonnaded ground, a summit bonfire was kept replenished by slaves bearing fuel up a gigantic interior spiral. The light of the flames, reflected and intensified by some shiny material still undefined, flashed outwards to warn of the low coastline whose reefs could all too easily impale ships driven fast by the dominant north wind.

Apart from handling the trade between the Roman mediterranean and the Indian east, Alexandria inherited the literary culture of Athens while developing to its highest extent the science which had first been cultivated in the Greek cities of the Aegean. The Pharos symbolised Alexandria. Its triune structure matched the city's division into three nations: Egyptians, Macedonians (or Greeks) and Jews. The groups which comprised the population of this Greek-speaking cosmopolis cohabited with no more mutual affection than the elements that comprise today's New York. The city's most impressive temple, the Serapeum, dominated the narrow lanes of Rakotis, the native quarter. It was dedicated to a god intended to link the mythologies of Egypt and Greece. But the Greek quarter, 'downtown Alexandria', lay to its east. It again anticipated Manhattan, its streets laid out in the gridiron pattern already adopted in several other late Greek cities. Its chief feature was two gigantic colonnaded highways which intersected at the tomb of Alexander. The city's youthful founder had been brought back from Iraq for interment at the heart of the city which summarised his achievement. The Greek sense of symmetry dominated, with its columns and porticos, the marble palace of the Ptolemies, the Library of the Mouseion and the temples of Poseidon and Isis. Although the Jews were hedged off from Egyptians and Greeks by their law, they occupied two of the city's five regions. Their sober, statueless streets, east of the marbled, fleshly splendours of the white Greek city, nurtured a life which could not remain permanently separate from that of their neighbours. Alexandrian Jews spoke and wrote Greek. They read their own scriptures in the Septuagint version. Many bore Greek names, either as nicknames attached to Hebrew names, or as names standing alone. Their most famous writer (a contemporary of Jesus[1]) bore the Greek name Philo. His father had been named Alexander, after the city's founder, while his nephew was, as Tiberius

---

[1] Born around BC 20 he died some time after AD 40.

Alexander, to play a leading role, on the Roman side, in the siege of Jerusalem.

In an Alexandrian context the names of Mary and her son would tell their own story. It would establish them as belonging to the Hellenistic culture of Egypt's major port. Mary may conceivably have been known as Miriam in her Galilean girlhood; the Koran invariably uses this form (the name of the sister of Moses and Aaron) on the many occasions she is mentioned, and the evangelists (see also Acts 1, 14) are inconsistent on this point, sometimes using one form, sometimes the other. This is not due to carelessness or even to ignorance, but points once again to the cultural division in Levantine society of the day between those who were touched by the international culture then prevailing, and those who were not; as also to that middle ground of government, finance, fashion, the army, commerce and pleasure, occupied by those who had a Jewish, Aramaic or Egyptian name at home and a Greek or even Latin one in public. For Maria was a name made fashionable in the Roman world after the triumph of Julius Caesar. It is the female form of Marius, a Roman statesman who had married an aunt of the future dictator, whose policies his own foreshadowed. A woman named Maria belonged as closely to a world dominated by Rome as a man named Cleopatros (or Clopas) belonged to a smaller world obedient to the Ptolemies.

So, whether Maria was Miriam in the homestead, or whether certain Jews or Jewish congregations preferred a Jewish usage, cannot be determined at this distance. Nor, by the same token, is there any evidence that Mary's son was ever known by any of the Semitic forms of Joshua, for which Jesus is the Greek equivalent,[1] during his lifetime. What is possible, however, is that while living in Egypt Jesus bore a second, purely pagan name as well as the Greek form of Joshua, his name in religion. This was as common practice among first-century Jews as it is today for a Levi who has westernised his name to Lewis also to be known by some gentile nickname such as Chuck. Among Greek-speaking contemporaries the young Jesus may well have been known as Chrêstos, a name popular for its connotations of good, or gentleness.[2]

[1] The same Hellenised form was used by two High Priests of the first century: Jesus son of Damnaos and Jesus son of Gamaliel.

[2] Although by this date few Egyptians could still read the hieroglyphic script of their ancestors, or its hieratic development, fortune-tellers and occultists will have found significance in a Greek name whose initial letters, X and P, could recall Khepera, 'The Creator of the Gods', and Rê, the Egyptian equivalent of Hêlios. When, much later, Chrêstos had been changed by his followers into the different but similar-sounding Christos, the first two letters, ☧, became the sacred monogram in catacomb inscriptions.

CHAPTER THREE

Mary

A picture of Jesus's origins begins to clarify. It is hardly surprising that it differs from that purveyed in Sunday school. Joseph, the father of children by a former wife[1], discovers, in Palestine, that the young girl to whom he is betrothed has been made pregnant by someone other than himself. Either, like many first-century Jews, he no longer adheres to the harsh laws of his faith or, in their despite, he heeds the kinder language of the heart.[2] He decides in any case to remove Mary from the tongues of the malicious. Since his family have business connections with Egypt, it is logical for him to select it as his place of exile. The country has, in Alexandria, the metropolis with the largest Jewish population in the empire and, at Leontopolis, the one sacrificing temple outside Jerusalem; Mary's child is born but a short distance from this important cult centre. Like other Jews and all native Egyptians, the baby is circumcised. Once Mary is fit to travel, they resume their journey to Alexandria and somewhere within the gigantic shadow of the lighthouse that dominates the harbour they stay, either with Joseph's brother Clopas, or in a house of their own.

By discarding as mythology most Christmas card details, we by no means devalue the youthful Mary. Priests, mostly celibate, were from the second century on to fashion, as the antidote to love on earth, a Queen of Heaven. Chaste, demure, obedient, her representations often recalling some waxwork doll, she was to be honoured for her role rather than anything positive in herself. The Davidic tower, the star of the sea, the second Eve: she was everything but a normal woman, let alone an individual as out of the ordinary as her son.[3]

Our Mary emerges, from the circumstances of the flight and the events she helped set in train, as a woman whose importance we can hardly exaggerate. An adolescent, perhaps fifteen, innocent but be-

[1] Mark names the sons – James, Joset, Jude and Simon – but not the daughters. Mark 6, 3.
[2] 'But . . . if the tokens of virginity be not found for the damsel: Then they shall bring out the damsel to the door of her father's house, and the men of her city shall stone her with stones that she die.' Deut. 22, 20–21.
[3] Cf. Marine Warner: *Alone of All Her Sex, The Myth and the Cult of the Virgin Mary*, London, 1976.

guiled, tough if socially abashed, surviving and determined that her
son should survive, we can see in her, once we sponge away the supernatural gloss and remove the trumpery jewels and the insipid smile,
the human being with the greatest influence on Jesus. On the battle-
field of exile she is to help form a personality of archetypal clarity who,
unphotographed, undescribed, imprecisely dated, nevertheless, like a
telexed press photo, comes across recognisably even if a dot here, or a
cluster of dots there, gets wrongly transmitted. For her to have been
responsible for the formation of so extraordinary a son we must posit a
woman as unlike the mass-produced statues of popular piety as Cleopatra was unlike some heavyweight Hollywood actress mimicking her
in a film. To conceive a son without a father's chromosomes, to mate
with a god were commonplace ideas in the Hellenistic east. They
remained an impressive 'miracle' to the puritanical and pre-scientific
age which lasted almost into living memory. But to form Jesus, even in
part, was an achievement of genius.

An only son tends to reflect, by imitation or intimate rejection, the
deepest characteristics of his mother. To infer therefore that Jesus was
some sort of image of his mother is a reasonable assumption. Her attitudes, accepted or questioned, were a lasting influence on his temperament and thus his life. It is here legitimate, for a very brief moment, to
examine the psyche of her son (which we know as we know characters
in fiction, not the two-dimensional canvases of the portrait artist), not
for what it tells about him, but for what it reveals about her. One incident is particularly relevant, both because it involves a situation akin to
her own when she became pregnant with Jesus, and because it shows
the personality of Jesus at its most distinctive. The story of the woman
taken in adultery belonged in none of the original gospel texts[1] but was
so evidently genuine that later editors inserted it into John.

> The scribes and Pharisees brought a woman along who had been
> caught committing adultery; and making her stand there in full view
> of everybody, they said to Jesus, 'Master, this woman was caught in
> the very act of committing adultery, and Moses has ordered us in the
> Law to condemn women like this to stoning. What have you to say?'
> They asked him this as a test, looking for something to use against

[1] In *The Gospel According to John*, The Anchor Bible, 1966, Raymond E. Brown
characterises the incident as a 'non-Johannine interpolation'. It appears in no early
Greek text of John, nor in the Coptic and Syriac versions. There is no reference to it by
any Greek theologian during the first Christian millennium, although Jerome included
it in the Vulgate. Some of its implications transcend the aspect that interests us here.
The narrative falls into two unequal parts. The public occasion, up to the clause 'until
Jesus was alone with the woman', has a more solid claim to depend on witnesses. Jesus
is not likely to have informed others what he said in private to the woman, whose state
of mind was undoubtedly confused. The command 'don't sin any more', is the sort of
thing an editor would find it prudent to add.

him. But Jesus bent down and started writing on the ground with his finger. As they persisted with their question, he looked up and said, 'If there is one of you who has not sinned, let him be the first to throw a stone at her.' Then he bent down and wrote on the ground again. When they heard this they went away one by one, beginning with the eldest, until Jesus was left alone with the woman, who remained standing there. He looked up and said, 'Woman, where are they? Has no one condemned you?' 'No one, sir,' she replied. 'Neither do I condemn you,' said Jesus; 'go away, and don't sin any more.'[1]

The incident illustrates radical elements in Jesus's personality. He feels unfettered by the strict law which the scribes and Pharisees quote correctly. His gesture recalls sand-writing, to this day an Egyptian form of magic. And he is strikingly compassionate. Augustine's beautiful summary – *relicti sunt duo, misera et misericordia* – loses in the English: 'two stay behind, the pitiful and pity.' Other stories reveal equally surprising traits which, perhaps along with many of his sayings, derive from Mary's attitudes or the things he remembered her saying to him when he was a boy. Puritans taunted him for enjoying wine – a pleasure which Mary encouraged him to provide for others on a notable occasion. He showed a readiness to be anointed with sweet-smelling unguents, a taste he shared not only with the prophet Muhammad but also middle eastern non-ascetics. His persistent curiosity about himself recalls T. E. Lawrence's hunger to have puzzling things about himself illuminated by other artists, in particular painters. Showing no false modesty, he compares himself to the bridegroom, which to this day has a peacock echo in everyday Arabic. He tells his disciples that while the poor are always with them, he will not be. The ikonography which links him to an instrument of torture should not blind us to his association in life with acts of gentleness, with flowers, birds, animals and, of course, children.

Hindus and Buddhists, it has been observed, recognise in Mary's son a personality which fits their conception of the sage. Yet, paradoxically, although Jesus was to become the god of the west, he has been hard to harmonise with the main strands of European tradition, whether found in Roman stoicism, the cerebral mandarinate of the French polytechnic, or the contrasted ideals of the Prussian aristocracy or the British public school. Western societies, when they produce men with even remote affinities to Jesus, tend to persecute them. India does not.

The author of a psycho-analytic study of Hindu culture and personality provides help towards solving the puzzle of this closeness to

[1] John 8, 3–11:JB.

Hindu norms, without postulating that Jesus visited India. Philip Spratt investigated the way in which the distinctive Hindu personality is created,[1] almost entirely by the mother. He asserts, in the jargon of his school, that the dominant Hindu type is narcissistic. 'In every psyche a certain quantum of libido is cathected[2] upon the ego. This condition is established in the first months of life, and some trace of it remains: this is called primary narcissism. But in some cases an abnormally big charge of libido is cathected on the ego. This is secondary narcissism.' By contrast, the psychic type in which much aggressiveness is directed against the ego is designated as punitive. 'In Europe the punitive personality is normal, the narcissistic exceptional; in India the narcissistic type is normal, the punitive exceptional.'[3] The mother creates and perpetuates this specific narcissistic personality. The punitive western super-ego (the Freudian substitute for the conscience) is formed from interiorised authoritative figures. 'The ego is spurred on by the super-ego, which is an unconscious image of the aggressive side of authority, especially the father; the super-ego draws its strength from the subject's own aggressiveness. The conscience is thus a charge of aggressiveness directed against the ego and forcing it to try to live up to its ideals. The emotion which it engenders is that of guilt.' This formation of guilt is inevitable since actual behaviour falls short of these ideals which these authoritative figures command.

It needs to be stressed that guilt differs from repentance, which is a rational response to an erroneous action. Guilt is a diffused, largely unconscious conviction that, in one's very existence as a human being under human pressures, one is inadequate, or even evil. Repentance is healthy; guilt is morbid. The three ideological bulwarks of western society, Hellenic, Roman, Hebrew, are cemented with guilt.

Yom Kippur, the day on which a Jew had to cleanse himself from sin and on which a scapegoat was thrown over a desert precipice,[4] manifests the centrality of guilt in Hebrew culture. The extraordinary persistence of its shoots and suckers is shown in the lives of those who consciously reject the Jewish religion. Paul is a classic instance. While the burden of his teaching was anti-nomian, he could not help positing a deity whose relationship to his creatures demanded a sacrificial victim. The guilt which percolated into Christianity through writers like Paul fostered the view of the sexual process as smeared with sin, and eventually demanded a saviour born of a mother untouched by

[1] Philip Spratt: *Hindu Culture and Personality, A Psycho-Analytic Study*, Bombay, 1966.
[2] Cathexis is a Freudian attempt to render Freud's term *Besetzung*; 'concentrated' would give the sense.
[3] Op. cit., p.6.
[4] Leviticus 16, 30.

man. The feminine role in sexual relations lay at the heart of original sin. In the doctrine of the Immaculate Conception, guilt was to push yet further than the notion of the Virgin Birth. This doctrine, defined in the nineteenth century, taught that while Mary had been begotten in the usual manner, she had been uniquely preserved from the taint affecting ordinary mortals.

The Jesus brought up by Mary was to manifest none of the punitive qualities labelled as anal by those who invented the psycho-analytic jargon. Forgiving and imaginative, tolerant, generous, indifferent to food taboos and ritual washing, healing by unhygienic methods which would affright a modern physician, he was to draw women to him in a society where they were generally regarded as men's inferiors.

How Mary shaped this remarkable son is a matter of conjecture, since all we have is the end result. Her conversation, her gestures, her opinions, must all have impressed him, sometimes to imitation, sometimes to rejection. For them to have done this in such a radical manner it seems probable that her influence was unsapped by a guilt-injecting paternal figure. This would have been the case if Joseph died early, exerted little influence in the home or, conceivably, returned to his other children in Galilee. Mary's own individuality seems to have sharpened in later life. At times she may have irked her son. There is no indication that she clung to Joseph's family. In the movement of ideas that followed her son's death she seems to have played no role among the factions who disputed its direction. Her absence from the letters of Paul (who visited the place of her traditional exile) is not to be ignored.

For this woman to have moulded so unusual a son, and to have herself preserved an independent character, a domicile uncrushed by traditional modes seems more likely than rural Galilee. Metropolitan Alexandria was the first century's nearest approximation to the anonymous modern city which makes or tolerates the heterodox individual.

CHAPTER FOUR

Childhood Without a Galilean Accent

For the boyhood of Jesus our sources between them offer one isolated incident: Luke's tale of him confounding his elders in the temple.
The story belongs in spirit with apocryphal tales of the infant wonder-
worker fashioning birds of clay which then fly off. If it has any basis in
fact, the incident could as well have taken place in Leontopolis as in
Jerusalem. Yet the notion that Jesus returned as an infant to Galilee
with his parents and assisted his apparent father in the carpenter's
shop has no stronger evidence. Even the evidence for Joseph being a
carpenter is meagre. The New Testament's two references to car-
pentry in fact amount to one. Mark gives the basic account when he
describes the amazement of the townspeople of Nazareth at the per-
formance of Jesus:

> Where did the man get all this? What is this wisdom that has been
> granted him, and these miracles that are worked through him? This
> is the carpenter surely, the son of Mary, the brother of James and
> Joset and Jude and Simon? His sisters, too, are they not here with
> us?[1]

Aramaic, the common language of Nazareth, is akin to both Hebrew
and Arabic. It imposes its own patterns on the Greek Mark used for his
gospel. The townsfolk describe the 'son of Mary' as 'the carpenter'.
The Greek word *tekton* renders the Aramaic *naggar*, which happens to
remain the colloquial Arabic word for carpenter in modern Egypt.
Matthew changes two small details: Jesus is referred to as 'the carpenter's son' (not 'the son of Mary') and the question becomes: 'Is not his
mother the woman called Mary?'[2] References to brothers and sisters
naturally troubled later churchmen. If Mary were their mother too,
the dogma of Mary's perpetual virginity would be undermined.
Matthew's concern with his hero's glory prompted him to move Jesus
some distance from the carpenter's bench.

Yet a Jewish writer on Jesus, Geza Vermes, has recently argued that

---

[1] Mark 6, 2–3: JB.
[2] Matthew 13, 55: JB.

naggar may not, in the context, have meant carpenter anyway.[1] Vermes notes that when differences in the Greek texts of the gospels do not indicate doctrinal difficulties they often reflect 'a linguistic problem in the expression in Hellenistic terms of something typically Jewish'. The difference over Mark's carpenter and Matthew's carpenter's son may be one such instance; on more than one occasion the Talmud uses the Aramaic *naggar* to designate a scholar or learned man, not a literal carpenter. The questions which Mark bunches together should perhaps be read antiphonally:

'Where on earth did this Jesus learn what he knows?'
'But he is Mary's learned son.'

The traditional sawdust and plane would then have to yield to the scholar's books and candle.

Does the gospel silence about his youth oblige us to accept the traditional picture of a childhood in Galilee? Mr Vermes, while questioning the tradition of Joseph's trade, accepts that Jesus was a lifelong resident of the northern province. His argument merits examination. 'The Jesus of the Gospels conforms to the specifically Galilean type. He is to begin with an appreciative child of the Galilean countryside. The metaphors placed in his mouth are mostly agricultural ones, as would be expected from a man who spent the major part of his life among farmers and peasants. For him the ultimate beauty is that of the lilies of the field, and the paradigm of wickedness the sowing of weeds in a cornfield, even in one belonging to an enemy. The city and its life occupy scarcely any place at all in his teaching. It is in fact remarkable that there is no mention whatever in the Gospels of any of the larger Galilean towns.'[2]

Yet the evidence in this passage can lead in the opposite direction. The picture of Jesus as a child of Galilee, the associate of farmers and peasants, like much in the Jesus story, has been enforced by painters. An analogous cliché, confirmed by a host of writers, long held that Muhammad was the child of the desert. But a modern biographer has convincingly established that this vision of a prophet inspired by desert storms and bedouin simplicity was largely false: Muhammad's revelation 'appeared not in the atmosphere of the desert, but in that of high finance'.[3] Do the metaphors of Jesus really prove him a Galilean? Jesus certainly responded to the beauty of flowers, but the best nature poetry has been written by townsmen. Theocritus, who invented the pastoral, spent his adult life in Alexandria having been brought up in

[1] Geza Vermes: *Jesus the Jew, A Historian's Reading of the Gospels*, London, 1973: p.21.
[2] Ibid, p.48.
[3] W. Montgomery Watt: *Muhammad at Mecca*, Oxford, 1953: p.3.

Syracuse, the chief city of Sicily. William Wordsworth is remembered for poetry inspired by the English lakeland; yet his formative years were spent in Cambridge, London, Switzerland and France. Thus when Jesus compares Solomon unfavourably with the lilies[1] of the field, he does not necessarily reveal a rural past.

The figurative language which Jesus uses in his parables is more certainly his than that of his isolated sayings. A skilful plagiarist can easily compose one or two verses in the manner of Swinburne or even Shakespeare, but would find it hard to fake a major body of short stories. The imagery used in the parables, the recurring themes, do provide clues to the years which had prepared Jesus for his mission. The metaphors do not certify a rural upbringing; and where the imagery is indeed rural it is not necessarily Galilean.

To take a few of the best known examples. One striking passage in which Jesus is describing the role of his disciples links three images drawn from experience:

> You are the light of the world. A city built on a hill-top cannot be hidden. No one lights a lamp to put it under a tub; they put it on the lamp-stand where it shines for everyone in the house.[2]

The light of the world is primarily the sun; but the image could have been inspired by the flaring Pharos lighting the channel into the Alexandrian harbour. The lampstand was something found in village house or town house throughout the empire. The city set on a hill hardly suggests Galilee, whose most imposing cities were by the lake shore.

In another parable, Jesus compares the man who heeds his words to

> the man when he built his house dug, and dug deep, and laid the foundations on rock; when the river was in flood it bore down on that house but could not shake it, it was so well built.

The man who listens but does nothing is compared to the man who builds his house on soil, with no foundations:

> as soon as the river bore down on it, it collapsed.[3]

Potamos, Luke's word for river suggests more than a Galilean torrent. The picture could apply as well to Alexandria as to Northern Palestine, or better. The Canopic branch of the Nile flowed beyond the eastern suburbs of the city and flooded with greater or less volume every summer. Alexandria owed its solidity to the limestone islets on which it was built.

[1] The lilies in question may have been the *Adonis anemone*, found in Cyprus, Lebanon and Egypt, as well as Palestine.
[2] Matthew 5, 14–16: JB.
[3] Luke 6, 46–49: JB.

The numerous parables to do with money, the pounds left with servants, the purchase of a valuable pearl, fit an urban, commercial background better than a farming community. The woman rejoicing over a lost coin, the man who runs out of bread at midnight and borrows three loaves from his friend, could easily be found in the back streets of a great city. The environs of Alexandria, half desert, half sown, could prompt images linked with farming, such as the lost sheep, or the sower who sowed on a mixture of soils. And the contention that Jesus never mentions one of the larger Galilean towns does not prove a village boyhood. It could better indicate that Jesus had not lived for a long period in Palestine. Even a country boy visits the local town. But a stranger from a metropolis as impressive as Alexandria might well not bother with the Galilean cities.

In later life most of his disciples were recruited from the northern province and on a key occasion the most prominent was identified by his Galilean accent.[1] If Jesus had spoken an Aramaic as uncouth to Judaeans as Glaswegian English to Londoners his enemies would surely have used it against him. The fact that no such accent is recorded makes it unlikely that he had one.

[1] Matthew 26, 73.

CHAPTER FIVE

The Intellectual Climate of His Young Manhood

The first-century Roman empire is better known to us than any other society before the age of printing. Its memorable literature and durable artifacts enable us to place Jesus in that particularity of objects and ideas which gives every man and woman much of their identity.

The triumph of Augustus, a generation earlier, had for the first time politically united the Mediterranean basin. At La Turbie, overlooking Monte Carlo, a spectacular monument records the suppression, by BC 6, of more than forty tribes which had previously disputed the mountain passes connecting Italy, France and the German south. Similar actions elsewhere had imposed a similar administration on territories stretching from western Europe as far east as Syria and Egypt. Italy and Greece, at the half-way point, had established cultural modes which dominated the empire as powerfully as those of England and France did the first two centuries of the United States of America. Regional differences intensified or weakened this Greco-Roman bond. Some border provinces were more open to extraneous infiltrations than others and produced a syncretic blend rather than conformity to an accepted standard. Syria acted as one bridge for ideas from the east, and in particular Persia. But the fleets that utilised the newly discovered monsoon for the voyage from the Red Sea to the Punjab diffused a knowledge of Indian attitudes and ideas. The Great Sahara, on the other hand, kept North Africa strictly Latin; although even there a subjugated population, part Semitic, part Berber, modified the mix.[1]

The dominant classical culture expressed itself in various forms, shaping some in the universalist ideals of Zeno the Stoic and others in the hedonism of Epicurus, while inclining yet others to react against the contagion of too much thought. Conservatives valued mindless traditions as barriers to the disintegration which threatens a pluralist society. But antagonists inside a century, however bitter their struggles, have more in common with each other than with their

---

[1] A mosaic memorial in a Tunisian museum is inscribed *Requiescat In Bace*. A difficulty in distinguishing *p* from *b* still troubles the Arabic-speaker.

forerunners or successors. All those who lived between the suicides of Cleopatra[1] and Nero[2] acted out their struggles before a backdrop of shared assumptions. Romans deplored the orientalisation of their society. 'Jews will sell you whatever dreams you like,' wrote a satirist, 'for a few small coppers.'[3] Jews opposed Hellenism with its all too human gods. But such opponents breathed a similar air and shared similar notions. Romans took serious note of dreams, omens and prodigies; Jews used classical motifs to embellish their synagogues. Few questioned that the planets influenced daily life, that devils caused illness and that the sun went round the earth. When Jesus was to speak of 'sun and moon and the powers of heaven', he was to use the language of his day.[4]

The revolutionary newness of the imperial structure was appreciated, or at least made use of, by its contemporaries, though many were aware of its faults. The official poet, Virgil, had written an eclogue whose messianic vision persuaded later Christians that he had predicted the birth of Jesus; but behind the solid bastions of imperial optimism (for Virgil had in mind a descendant of Augustus) a melancholy torrent flows into view. The poet gives his last epic lines to a pre-Roman warrior whose defeat symbolises the disintegration of the smaller communities of the past. At the other extreme, Jewish hostility to the cosmopolitan empire was accompanied by an undertone of admiration. The best Jewish minds of the age embraced aspects at least of the pagan culture.

To our loss, but not our surprise, much of the empire's detritus has perished. Rome's gazette, perhaps the first daily newspaper in history, survives only in its name, the *Acta Diurna*. If a copy were to be recovered, it would tell us about urbane patricians. But the surviving works of satirists and historians push fingers of light into the capital's tenements. We hear the heavy unsprung wagons, forbidden the city in the daytime hours, grinding their raucous nocturnal passage. Painters, sculptors and architects help us to picture the existence of those who wore the toga or the citizen's tunic. Poets take us into their minds and novelists preserve their loves, or infatuations.

Rome itself was torn by social conflict. The senatorial patricianate exemplified by Marcus Brutus, assassin of Caesar, was to be superseded by the city proletariat who, in the spirit of Argentina's shirtless Peronistas, supported the populists of Caesar's house. In the Levant, an overriding conflict had sprung from the tension between two articulate peoples, each with an exalted opinion of its merits. At one pole, the

[1] BC 30.
[2] AD 68.
[3] Juvenal: *Satire* 1, 547; tr. Peter Green.
[4] Mark 13, 25; Matthew 24, 29; Luke 21, 26.

Greeks had created cultural platforms from which they defined non-Hellenists as barbarians. At another, observant Jews hugged themselves as the custodians of a revelation which instructed them to avoid *ha-goyyim*, the gentiles. 'You only have I known of all the families of the earth.' So Yahweh addresses Israel through his prophet Amos.[1]

Few Levantines existed at either extreme. First-century Hellenism had become the property of a mixed multitude of diverse peoples. They spoke and wrote a colloquial Greek, the *koinê*, which broke the grammatical rules of Pericles and Plato. Not many prayed to the Olympian gods with conviction. The Ptolemies had invented Serapis in the glare of history so as to unite Nilotic Egyptians with immigrant Hellenes. Combining qualities of Osiris and Jupiter, the new deity was shown supporting a basket of mysteries on the tangled locks of a riverine god. Most Jews since the dawn of the Persian era stood at some distance from the primitive ideas of Moses and Samuel. Along with the cult of angels they had absorbed the Iranian vision of the world as an arena between good and evil. For several centuries the particularist notion of Yahweh as the god of Israel had been shading into a more universalist notion of the god of heaven. So once again Jesus would be of his time in 'raising his eyes to the sky' when starting a particularly solemn prayer.[2] Jews were impressed by Greek intellectual prestige and the Greek vocabulary, subtler and richer than Hebrew or its close relative, the everyday Aramaic of Palestine. This had accepted hundreds of Greek loan words: Geza Vermes confirms that macaronic – the use by one speaker of several languages at once – was as common as in modern Lebanon. 'A mixture of Aramaic and Greek would have been more or less intelligible to most Jews in the first century AD.'[3] The language of the gospels uses terms like Hades freely.[4]

If Jesus had been born a century sooner, he would, in Palestine, have owed allegiance to an autonomous Jewish polity, or in Egypt to a Hellenistic empire. Born under Augustus, he lived and died the subject of a military state directed from the Italian peninsula. The organisation through which Rome manifested its distinctive genius was attested in such details as the disciplined lettering of its inscriptions or, more basically, in durable roads and rational laws. The urban background to the life of Jesus, whether in Alexandria or Jerusalem, was formed by the standards of taste the Romans had made theirs. But despite Rome's power to switch its legions urgently from one threatened province to another, its triumph was shallow and impermanent. Its Hellenism was a bridge over a tide whose course was changing.

[1] Amos 3, 1–2.
[2] John 17, 1: DS.
[3] Op. cit., p. 113.
[4] Cf. Luke 16, 23.

Alexander the Great, the pupil of Aristotle, had projected Greek culture into the east, founding Hellenic cities, diffusing Hellenistic sculpture as far as Afghanistan and northern India – only for Hellenism to be sapped by the forces it conquered. After the first three Ptolemies, the Macedonian dynasty directing Egypt had lost the qualities which true Greeks admired. Its powerful successor, Roman paganism, had the spiritual vitality of a *papier mâché* giant. The Romans had assimilated the Olympian gods to their own, identifying Aphrodite with Venus and Pallas Athene with Minerva. Their empire was studded with temples distinguished by the height and order of their columns or their quantities of sculpted foliage. But they satisfied the human soul as little as a modern airport. The very success of the empire had emptied most Greek temples of awe. Paid magistrates performed periodic rites in their pillared gloom; an equivalent of a ministry of works maintained their fabric.

The system's inability to answer spiritual demands came when such demands were suddenly insistent. The Greek religious system had filled the chinks in the life of the city-state, a life so active and articulate that it was only in moments of frustration or death that most people felt the need for heavenly consolation. But the triumph of Rome meant the absorption of independent cities, just as it foreboded the destruction of Jewish control over their own affairs. The first half of Karl Marx's aphorism on religion is less quoted than the second: 'religion is the sigh of the soul in a soulless world.' Untrue in the city-state, it accurately reflects the spiritual plight of the Roman empire. A city-state gave the illusion of home to men and women in a cosmos which was otherwise cruel. Some such states were ruled by tyrants, a few by popular assemblies, many by a mafia of the rich. Since a man could wheedle a tyrant, stand for election or bribe an oligarch, he could be spiritually healthy under all three systems. If he failed, he did so in a personal context. A letter to the third Ptolemy, a despot in the old Greek sense, has been recovered from the sands of Egypt. It is from a Greek who signs his name baldly as Antigonos. It can be dated to about BC 233 and gives the flavour of a still personal state:

> To King Ptolemy, Greeting. Antigonos. I am being unjustly treated by Patron, the superintendent of police in the lower toparchy.[1]

This man-to-man communication shows the persistence of the unservile spirit – though it was probably confined to the Greek-speaking caste. Antigonos would fight for King Ptolemy in an emergency and the ruler was expected to remedy his complaint. But these early Ptolemies were succeeded by lesser descendants who compensated for

[1] H. Idris Bell: *Egypt from Alexander the Great to the Arab Conquest*, Oxford, 1948: p. 125.

their lack of intrinsic worth by faking the awe of the pharaohs.

The empire fashioned by Augustus had abolished any intimacy between ruler and ruled. For the first time mediterranean man knew cosmic loneliness. The *Annals* of Tacitus, the empire's greatest historian and one of the first Roman historians to mention Jesus, 'convey the reader through a bleak land, without light or hope. "Humanitas" and "integritas", obsolete equipment, have long been discarded; while "veritas" and "prudentia" now cease to have any value. Fear holds domination, or fraud; what abides for ever is discord and tyranny.'[1] The only temples with any meaning were erected to Rome and Augustus. For deeper aspirations Caesar's subjects looked to the east. All classical society, from the richest senator to the most abject slave, felt this eastern pull. Only two years after defeating Antony and Cleopatra, Augustus decreed the removal of temples of Serapis and Isis outside Rome's limits. Yet such measures availed little. Half a century later, his heir Tiberius was issuing new orders for the dismantling of the temple of Isis and for orientals, including Jews, to be expelled from the City.

The decay of Hellenic paganism was sensed most acutely by the Hellenes themselves. Antipater of Thessalonika was an exact contemporary of Jesus. His poems contrast sourly with the great themes of early Greece. One degrades Zeus, who had wooed Danae in a shower of stars, to a lecher buying a whore with Roman coins:

A golden age there was. A bronze. A silver,
Once. But Kytherea interlinks the three,
Honouring the gold man and the brassy
Without, of course, disdaining him of silver.
Venus is Nestor-old. Zeus to Danae
Came as the bringer of a hundred sovereigns.

Antipater equates love, the idealised topic at Plato's dinner-party, with orgasmic potency:

For us men the span of our poor lives is brief,
Even if we could all expect old age. Our prime is briefer.
Thus, while time is fresh, let it pour over:
Song, sex, debauches. Soon comes weighty winter.
Then not even a thousand drachmas
Will help you come. Impotence awaits you.[2]

Insatiably curious, with a sometimes overlooked taste for the irrational, the Greeks were fascinated by the Egypt where they had made

[1] *Tacitus*: Ronald Syme; 2 vols, Oxford, 1958: p. 545.
[2] This author's translation. For text see *The Garland of Philip*, ed. A. S. F. Gow & D. L. Page, Cambridge, 1968.

their greatest scientific discoveries. They, and not the Egyptians for whom he was invented, paid chief cult to the god Serapis. (They took him far afield: his statues have been found all over the Empire.) They commandeered Egyptian mythology with the energy their forefathers had devoted to taking over the country.

To the Egyptians, the Greeks were one of the many peoples who were to enslave them. They had already experienced Persian occupation and in due course would take orders from Arabs, Turks and Englishmen. But the thousand years of Greek domination, from Alexander the Great to the coming of Islam, did most to sap their cultural vitality. If the Greeks had tried to suppress Rê and Isis, the fellahin might have found foci for resistance in their ancient temples. Instead, their masters enthused over the mysteries of Memphis and Thebes and used their intellectual systems to rationalise and develop a religion whose intuitive sense of symbol had been its strength. The Egyptians were left with an emotional void. They lost faith in their former gods and comprehension of their written tongue. The process had already begun when the priests or tourist guides at Giza gave Herodotus inexact information. In part, they sought rewards for tall stories; in part, they were genuinely ignorant of the past they claimed to expound. Their tales of Cheops, one-time tenant of the largest pyramid, present a garbled account of the heretical Akhnaton, the father-in-law of Tutankhamun. The cult of Ptah, the thinker-god of Memphis, had long been abandoned. The colours used in tombs changed from the greens and yellows of hope to the black and scarlet appropriate to Anubis, the sinister fox-god of death. Egyptian religion had gone, literally, underground. Sunlit Heliopolis, with its courtyards centring on obelisks, its communities of learned men, yielded to dark rites conducted in pits beneath the sand. In place of the calm majesty of early sculptures, grotesque figurines conferred potency on oneself and blight on one's enemies. For more than a thousand years papyrus copies of the Book of the Dead, magnificently illustrated, had been placed inside coffins. By the time of Jesus the Book's prayers, formulae and spells had dwindled to hieroglyphic squiggles of purely magical use.

Greek awareness of the emptiness of Olympian religion, Egyptian alienation from a system older than the pyramids, were accompanied by a general transference of attention from this world to the next: from the known to the exotic; from the measurable to the speculative. The afterlife of ancient Egypt had been this world prolonged; the new visions were gaseous and tormented. A major response to the horror of this life was the diffusion of mystery cults from the Levant to the west. Some involved Isis and Osiris, others the sun who in the person of the youthful Mithras defeats the bull of darkness. However disparate their symbols, the new common language, the Greek *koinê*, facilitated their progress.

The mysteries were neither frivolous nor cheap. They attracted brilliant minds as well as simple. They cost their practitioners time and money. The cultists of Isis needed a set of special white garments while Mithras was worshipped in structures gouged from the rock and rarely holding more than a hundred. The mysteries conferred few earthly advantages, though their priests showed the customary greed of ecclesiastics. But they united their members in a brotherhood superseding older ties of local pride. At their best, the cults represented an advance from the amoral folklore of Olympus. Many participants achieved spiritual elevation.

Yet a common disadvantage left these cults incomplete and open to replacement. A question hung over their central figures: had Isis ever existed? Was Mithras an entity living somewhere in the cosmos? Or were both mere symbols? Such questions had been asked about the gods as early as the reign of Alexander. An Egyptian priest had then explained to the youthful invader that gods and heroes were originally mortals who had then been raised to godhead. Such a theory was ultimately destructive of faith in the pagan gods. It was carried further under Ptolemy I when Hecataeus, a sceptical philosopher, asserted that the gods worshipped on earth were originally heavenly bodies, such as the Sun and the Moon. 'The gods, such as Zeus and Isis, had been men and women divinised because of their beneficent deeds to mankind.'[1]

Doubts about the historicity of the central figures inclined the addicted to change from one mystery to another, in the way modern faddists switch from a favourite guru to a macrobiotic diet. The new class structure helped the spread of such other-worldly cults. Julius Caesar and his family had won power by rallying the plebeians against the conservative aristocracy with its stern, old-fashioned code; the urban masses for whom they built amphitheatres of cruel amusement were unattracted by dutiful sobriety. When young and strong, they sought wealth and erotic success; when old or sick they sought personal survival. The change is symbolised in two Latin nouns: the conservative called their own ideas *religio* while damning as *superstitio* the ideas of the majority. *Superstitio* could find expression in a mystery cult or a visit to a fortune-teller. To the *religio* of a republic ruled by men like Brutus, Jupiter conveniently represented eternal order. But the new popular power was *Tychê*, or in Latin, *Fortuna*. An empire whose master lurked in a palace or seaside villa seemed ruled by chance, not intelligible design. A belief that the conjunctions of the stars ruled human fortunes was general while a solar monotheism influenced the

[1] S. Angus: *The Mystery Religions and Christianity*, London, 1925: p. 107.

more discerning. But neither the Sun's rhythmic link with changing seasons nor the assumptions of human impotence implicit in astrology could impose moral demands of any stringency, or give the strength to obey them.

In this Levantine world the Jews held an ambiguous position. Most of what we know about first-century Judaism derives from writings composed after the defeat of the Jewish revolt in AD 70. The Talmud, in its two compilations, provides one important miscellany, in its earliest texts deriving from around the end of the second century. An earlier and individual account comes from the historian, Flavius Josephus. The rabbis of the Talmudic tradition and the pro-Roman Josephus write from very different viewpoints. The Talmud collects the teachings of the scholars who salvaged Judaism from a Jerusalem surrendered to official paganism; their devoted labours enabled it to survive, without a sacrificing temple and outside Palestine. Josephus wished to improve the reputation of a people who were unpopular and defeated. In both cases there is an obvious danger of taking idealised, defensive accounts as literal depictions of what Judaism had been in its days of autonomy. Some first-century Jews clung to every detail of their ancient law, but many more did not. An island in the Nile provides hard evidence that for a long time Jews had been far from consistently monotheistic. In the early sixth century BC the Persians had established a colony of Jewish mercenaries on Elephantine Island near the modern Aswan. Employed by the Persians to guard the first cataract, they constructed a five-gated temple. Excavated in modern times, this temple proves that the colony honoured more than one god. While one portal was dedicated to Ya'u (or Yahweh), the four others seem to have been dedicated to Aneth, Bethel, Ishua and Herem. The fact that these four deities derived from Canaan and Syria, not from Egypt, shows that at that time the local religion exercised no attraction on the Asiatic Hebrews. This temple was finally destroyed by the native population. Animal sacrifices seem to have displeased the Egyptians while the polluting of fire outraged the Persians.[1]

By the time of Jesus Jews were drawn to a wide range of non-Hebraic ideas. One example is provided by an episode which is sometimes taken to typify Israeli tradition. When at Massada, in the last phase of the revolt, Eliezer exhorted his remaining soldiers to kill first their families, then themselves, he could find no argument in the Torah for such mass suicide. It was impossible for a Jew fighting Rome to invoke the deaths of Brutus or Seneca. According to Josephus, Eliezer invoked

those Indians who profess the exercise of philosophy; for these brave

[1] Cf. H. Idris Bell: *Cults & Creeds in Graeco-Roman Egypt*, Liverpool, 1953.

men do but unwillingly undergo the time of life, and look upon it as a necessary servitude, and make haste to let their souls loose from their bodies; nay, when no misfortune presses them to it, nor drives them upon it, these have such a desire of immortality, that they tell other men beforehand that they are about to depart; and nobody hinders them, but every one thinks them happy men, and gives them letters to be carried to their familiar friends that are dead: so firmly and certainly do they believe that souls converse with one another in the other world. So when these men have heard all such commands that were to be given them, they deliver their body to the fire; and, in order to their getting their soul a separation from the body, in the greatest purity, they die in the midst of hymns of commendations made to them; for their dearest friends conduct them to their death more readily than do any of the rest of mankind when they are going on a very long journey, who, at the same time, weep on their own account, but look upon the others as happy persons, as so soon to be made partakers of the immortal order of beings. Are we not, therefore, ashamed to have lower notions than the Indians?[1]

If ideas about Hindu thought, however idealised, had penetrated Judaea by AD 70, or at the time when Josephus wrote his *Wars of the Jews*, it is not surprising if Jewish contemporaries of Jesus were drawn to the mystery cults of nearby Egypt.

The pagan world was similarly divided in its attitude to the Jews. Romans regarded their distinctive practice of circumcision as uncouth. (Some Jews anxious to compete in pagan games reacted to this attitude by submitting to a painful operation which gave them the simulacrum of a foreskin.) Senior officials like Pontius Pilate would have agreed with the Juvenal who, satirising converts, gives a cold outsider's view of the Jewish religion:

Some, whose lot was to have Sabbath-fearing fathers,
Worship nothing but clouds and the *numen* of the heaven,
And think it as great a crime to eat pork, from which their parents
Abstained, as human flesh. They get themselves circumcised
And look down on Roman law, preferring instead to learn
And honour and fear the Jewish commandments, whatever
Was handed down by Moses in that arcane tome of his.

Such traditionalists as Juvenal, equally hostile to Greeks and Egyptians, were xenophobic rather than anti-Semitic.

Judaism intrigued many searchers in Alexandria, where the east was close and the Septuagint available. Monotheism itself was neither new

[1] Josephus: *Wars of the Jews*, Book VII, Chapter 8; tr. William Whiston.

nor the main attraction. Zarathustra, the Iranian prophet, had believed in one god, even if his priestly successors had restored the
dualism so fundamental to Iran. Early Egyptian texts, older by far than
the writings of Akhnaton, reflect a monotheistic view of creation.
What was more original in the Jewish scriptures was their attitude to
time. The Greeks saw time as circular and the primal act in this particular cycle was not creation but a reordering of matter. This view,
argued by an intellectual minority but instinctively supported by
millions, found a total contrast in a Jewish sense of time which
may be characterised as linear and purposeful. In other words,
while the Greeks saw no cosmic point of departure or arrival,
the Jews saw human history as something like a highway. Yahweh
had created the world and was working through history to an end of his
devising. Time was, indeed, the particular medium through which
Yahweh showed himself expressing his purpose through a chain of
spokesmen as well as through a sequence of events, some chastening,
some glorious. This historical highway would ultimately lead to a
millennial conclusion.

Judaism's attitude to time stamped its liturgical year, three major
feasts commemorating supposedly historical events. The spring Passover was linked with the night in which the Angel of the Lord slew the
firstborn of the Egyptians. The late winter feast of Purim recorded the
deliverances of Persian Jews from a hostile tyrant. The mid-winter
feast of Hanukka memorialised the defeat of the Seleucid empire in BC
160. It was unimportant that, except for the last event, these happen-
ings were probably mythical, or that Passover disguised the substitu-
tion of animal for human sacrifice. What mattered was the vision of
human destiny which such a view imposed on its adherents. For these
past events were imagined as anticipating a momentous event in the
future, the coming of a national deliverer with an apocalyptic mission.

The idea of such a messianic deliverer is not, of course, specifically
Jewish. James Henry Breasted, the historian of ancient Egypt, quotes
Ipuwer, a pharaonic sage living in the anarchic period following the
collapse of the Old Kingdom, for the earliest messianic text to be discovered anywhere.[1] Any troubled society is likely to dream of a deliverer. The Hellenistic world had shown traces of messianism in public
attitudes to Julius Caesar and other members of his dynasty, not
excluding Nero.[2] But for national messianism to be more than a phase,

[1] James Henry Breasted: *Development of Religion and Thought in Ancient Egypt*, New
York, 1912: pp. 211–212.
[2] Athenians applauded Julius Caesar as 'Saviour and Benefactor'; an inscription from
Halicarnassus terms Augustus 'Saviour of the whole human race'; while as late as AD
67 an altarpiece honours 'Nero God the Deliverer for ever': S. Angus, op.cit., p. 227.
Josephus saw Vespasian as filling a messianic role for the empire.

the nation involved must be cohesive and its problems persistent. The Egyptians were as cohesive as the Jews but their problems were recurrently solved. Ipuwer's dream of a man destined to restore Egyptian order had been achieved by the pharaohs of the Middle Kingdom. The problems of the Roman empire were to persist until its fall but its populace lacked cohesion. The Jews, by contrast, had a unity deliberately intensified by a law restricting contacts with gentile society. At the same time, the dream of establishing a powerful state in Palestine's narrow yet strategic limits produced persistent friction with their neighbours. There were varied notions of what the messiah would be, but most Jews seem to have hoped that Yahweh would send a deliverer from the house of David who would subjugate the heathen nations to his holy people.[1] The countries of the Levant which had lost their own independence to Rome knew of Jewish messianism. But while it aroused their interest, its ethnic limitations ruled out their support or participation. Later, however, the longing for a saviour was to be shown by the speed with which, in the second century, the Hellenistic world adopted a cosmopolitan variant of the messianic dream. The fact that it linked this idea of a supernatural intervention in human history with Jesus does not prove that it was the view which Jesus held himself, or that messianic ideals were parcel of his programme.

For the Greek and Jewish ideas of time were not to monopolise the intellectual arena. A third view began to affect western thought around the first century. In this view time was neither circular nor linear but basically meaningless. The origins of what was a feeling more than a precise philosophy cannot be precisely extricated, although Persian and Indian ideas must have played a role. Yet whatever its sources, a new mood began to challenge the Greek view of human action as inherently this-worldly, yet set in a frame of ultimate nihilism, and the Jewish view of things as moving to a temporal fulfilment. Champions of this third view often shared the Jewish contempt for pagan culture while arguing that the Jewish notion of development was invalid, too. The way to spiritual liberation was not through an external intervention which would rectify the pattern of human existence on earth, but in the vertical ascent of the soul to the real world which was its home. As against the separation between past and future, it posited a separation between higher and lower, between the states of this world and the kingdom of heaven. Those thinking on these lines pondered, not how to re-order this planet, but how to escape it. Some found the solution in the repudiation of the body and its claims. Opposed to such ascetics were libertines. They saw the answer in a liberating acceptance of the flesh. But to others, the gnostics, it lay in a particular species of knowledge.

[1] Cf. Psalm 17.

Gnosis, as a species of knowledge which confers liberation, even immortality, had had its prime proponent in Plato, the greatest of the pagan philosophers. Right knowledge, he had taught, was the supreme good, the precondition of right action. By the first two centuries of our era a gnostic was someone who claimed to possess this knowledge and who believed that gnosis, not the actions of a man himself or a saviour, conferred salvation. The name of gnostic would be claimed by adherents ranging from the insane to the sober, from the debauched to the saintly, and was no more precise than other vogue terms in other centuries. But fashion can traverse distances more swiftly than articulated theories.

Excavations near the Dead Sea have, since the Second World War, confirmed ancient accounts of the Essenes, a Jewish sect dissatisfied with the temple cult in Jerusalem. Even if some of their ideas derived from alien sources, the Essenes were as Jewish as the Pharisees. Their desert outpost stood at a similar angle to Judaism as monastic movements to Catholicism or later still, puritan sects to Islam.

Although some of the texts recovered from their long hidden library seem to echo sayings recorded by the gospel-writers (or their editors), the ethnocentric asceticism of the Dead Sea sect does not fit with the teaching and temperament of Jesus, whose liking for wine and whose willingness to associate with sinners of both sexes provided fuel for his critics. Another sect, established on the outskirts of Alexandria, seems much more likely to have influenced his youth. These were the Therapeutae, whose name has been variously interpreted as 'physicians' or 'attendants on God'. No physical remains of their settlement have so far been found, but we know of them from a treatise by Philo of Alexandria, a contemporary of Jesus.[1] Since his writings on the Essenes have been confirmed by the Dead Sea excavations, it is even more likely that he was accurate when writing about the Therapeutae, established as they were close to where he lived. Philo composed a diptych round the two movements which is known by its Latin title *De Vita Contemplativa*.[2]

To Philo, rather surprisingly, the Essenes stood for the practical life, growing crops and making things with their hands whereas the Therapeutae stood for the life of meditation, devoting their lives to reading and prayer.

The Therapeutae lived, more as hermits than monks or nuns, in the

[1] Philo, born in BC 20 into the highest Jewish class and devoted (except on one occasion in the reign of Caligula) to bookish pursuits, writes in an abstract manner about the Therapeutae, naming none of their leaders. It would not be surprising, if he had been an annalist, which he was not, that he named none of the disciples who were influenced by these universalist ascetics.

[2] *De Vita Contemplativa:* Introduction & Notes, F. Daumas; tr. P. Miquel, Paris, 1963.

undulant half-desert to the south-west of Lake Mareotis, across the water from Alexandria. The visitor who approaches the coastline from the sallow desert today comes on a long, low range of sandy hills. Camps whose military buildings date from the North African campaigns of the Second World War face a lake become saline since a British force destroyed the dykes in the early nineteenth century and let in the sea. The effluent of chemical and petroleum works have given the water a purplish, aniline hue. Similar scenery extends to the west of Alexandria where the ruined pharaonic temple of Taposiris stands by the sea; groves of succulent figs have been uprooted to make room for seaside villas. Remove the congested villas, the soldiers thumbing lifts to the city and the military buildings and there remain the long low intrusions of rain-watered hills between the desert to the south and the maritime metropolis which faces southern Europe. The cells of the vanished Therapeutae were probably similar to the houses which the bedouin build today, lured to the fringe of the city by the possibility of finding work. But, in grouping their cells in a community, the sect seems to have been inspired by the pious men whose decayed quarters had been noted by Strabo, the Greek geographer, some twenty-five years before the birth of Jesus. According to Philo, the Therapeutae focused their lives on prayer. At the climax of their assemblies some presiding sage would lecture them on holy writ, probing beneath its surface for an inner meaning. Philo himself did more than anyone else to popularise the method of studying scripture, not in the context of the time when it was written or the original writer's intentions, but for the allegorical constructions that could be fitted on to it.[1]

The latest editor of Philo's treatise has described where the Therapeutae differed from the Essenes.[2] While both groups preferred the desert or country, the Essenes could still live in towns. The Essenes had their chief establishment on a small plateau where the high cliffs of the Judaean mountains overlook the Dead Sea. The Therapeutae, as we have seen, colonised a bluff between Lake Mareotis and the sea. While postulants of both communities renounced private property, the Therapeutae seem to have assigned their goods to their relations, on the understanding that these persons would remit them enough for their needs; the Essenes used the property of individuals to support their community. Both sects observed the Sabbath and, except for one category of Essene, all practised continence and obedience. They dressed and fed as austerely as the very poor. They alike ate sacred

---

[1] 'The allegorical method enabled writers to link the present with the past; it could bring any ritual or drama into line with current ethics. It utterly ignored the intention of the writer or the original and obvious significance of a mystery ceremonial, and replaced these by the reader's or observer's own interpretation.' Angus, op.cit., p. 50.
[2] Op.cit., pp. 55–8.

meals in common, the Essenes preceding theirs with purificatory ablutions. Both despised the logic, rhetoric and physics of the secular
educational curriculum, believing these subjects contributed nothing
to virtue. But while the Essenes were nationalistic to the point of fanaticism, the Therapeutae professed a universalist philosophy in
harmony with the ideas of the Second Isaiah or Zeno the Stoic. Proclaiming themselves citizens of the world, open to outside ideas, the
Therapeutae regarded women as the equals of men, unlike the Essenes
who preserved the misogynism of the rabbis. At one night festival men
and women performed a choral dance. Yet on principle they did not
marry or beget children, seeking to have spiritual progeny only. While
the Essenes were commonly elderly men, the Therapeutae recruited
youths with a view to forming their character. The Therapeutae cared
nothing for eschatology or the hope of a messiah.

The diet of the Therapeutae was even more austere than that of the
Essenes. Their one concession to luxury was to add hyssop to their
coarse bread and salt at their weekly Sabbath. This seems a link with
the solar cult of Heliopolis, where hyssop had been popular with the
devotees.[1] Another link was the manner in which they began their
day. At dawn, like the praying Egyptians, they held their hands aloft
to the rising sun.

Where Jesus spent his boyhood must ultimately remain a matter for
speculation. But that it was somewhere in the Levant is almost certain
and no region there was immune to first-century ideas, though they
will have clashed more distinctly in Egypt than rustic Galilee. If he
spent part or all of his youth in Alexandria, it is likely that he frequen-
ted the Therapeutae. For long before he knew what his destiny was to
be, he will have been attracted to those with possible answers to the
questions which were to engross him later. Just as the future composer
is drawn to the piano more than the football, Jesus will have been
drawn to the community of dedicated men and women across the lake
from the commercial city. His adult attitude to life was to be closer to
that of the Therapeutae than to any other contemporary group of
whom we know.

---

[1] Porphyry's *De Abstinentia* (IV,6) quotes Chaeremon the Stoic for a description of
the last phase of communal life at Heliopolis.

CHAPTER SIX

His Parables As Clues To
His Experience

If there is no proof that Jesus spent all or part of his youth in Egypt, our hypothesis is more than idle guesswork. Admittedly we have no direct evidence of a documentary nature. (Such evidence would be equally hard to find for most of his contemporaries.) The contents of the Jewish record and notarial office[1] which seems to have existed in his lifetime have long since been dispersed; and while some census returns have survived on Egyptian papyrus, they do not refer to the edict which allegedly drew Joseph to Bethlehem. So far as we know, Jesus wrote nothing himself. The contributions of apocryphal gospels and the like are too late and too fanciful to be of biographical value. Except for the one brief incident in Luke, the four gospels are silent on his youth and the Roman historians who referred to him in the early years of the second century were uninterested in his development or motivation. They saw him as a malefactor whose followers disturbed the imperial peace.

Yet this lack of direct evidence does not leave us without clues, the most important of which derive from Jesus himself. For the imagery a man uses, even in his conversation, often reveals much of his background. And far richer than the figures of speech in his isolated sayings – which could have been prompted by several regions of the middle east – are his parables. These give indications, if nothing more, that Jesus was a stranger to, or prolonged absentee from, the Galilee where he was to start his mission.

Like other forms of imaginative literature, the parables draw on their author's deepest experience. Anyone who composes plays, novels, stories or essays tends to return to certain material and to intrude it, despite the precise situation of his characters or the development of his argument, when that material has particular resonance to him. Such private obsessions, much more than tricks of language, differentiate him from his contemporaries. The theme of treachery, for

[1] Cf. H. Idris Bell: op.cit., p.35.

instance, runs like a black thread through Shakespeare's work. Not that treachery was uncommon in an age which saw the young Elizabeth led through Traitor's Gate and in which those convicted of treason were disembowelled in public. Yet the Sonnets plainly indicate that an act of personal betrayal formed an agonising part of his private experience. Again, as has often been remarked, Queen Gertrude's account of Ophelia's death intrudes sexual references out of keeping with the scene which testify to the abundant libido of the author. The themes which recur in other writers' work are similarly revealing. If we lacked contemporary descriptions of D.H. Lawrence, we could still infer that the author of *Woman in Love* had a beard and narrow buttocks from his repeated attribution of these features to the heroes of his tales.

What indications do his parables provide of the experiences of Jesus in his first three decades?

Pithy maxims based on observation need not reveal any remarkable experience, though naturally they illumine an attitude to life. When Jesus contrasts the coin offered by a poor widow with the ostentatious alms of a pious worshipper, we infer that he had observed what went on in the Jerusalem temple; but this fact adds little substance to his biography.[1] The same is true even of some of the more complex parables. The story Jesus tells of the good Samaritan confirms his close knowledge of the intricate Jewish law.[2] The story has as its pivot the clash between the claims of charity, honoured by a despised Samaritan, and the law, which ruled that contact with a corpse was a cause of pullution which, in the case of the clergy, made them temporarily ineligible for tithes. The religious men who passed by on the other side were uncertain whether the robbed wayfarer was dead or alive. If dead, they would be polluted by approaching his corpse.

Jesus had undoubtedly walked the twisting, arid road up from the Jordan valley. To go further and argue that he himself was once waylaid, like the traveller in his story, or that like the Samaritan he had rescued a victim of thieves, would be an unwarranted speculation. But other parables exhibit patterns that seem etched by experience. The absentee, whether merchant, landlord or master, is a recurrent character in Jesus's stories. A property-owner living far from home plays a structural role in the parables of the talents (or pounds in some modern versions), the wicked vinedressers and the unjust steward. The archetypal structure of these stories can be considered separately from the teaching which the stories are intended to convey.

[1] Mark 12, 41–44; Luke 21, 1–4.
[2] As J. Duncan M. Derrett convincingly expounds in *Law in the New Testament*, London, 1974.

The parable of the talents has interesting variants in the three synoptics. None necessarily implies a Galilean provenance.

Mark's version is terse:

> Be on your guard, stay awake, because you never know when the time will come. It is like a man travelling abroad: he has gone from home, and left his servants in charge, each with his own task; and he has told the door-keeper to stay awake.[1]

The general counsel to wakefulness[2] is linked to a man who has servants and travels.

Matthew treats of a capitalist who has deposited varying sums with his servants and later rewards those who have used them wisely.[3] Luke, more exotically, writes of a patrician summoned abroad to take up the position of king but compelled, because of the hatred of his compatriots, to return. The man (the story is somewhat obscure) apparently retains the power to reward or promote those whose investments he approves.[4]

The parable of the wicked vinedressers, our second example, involves a landowner who plans a vineyard. Since vines normally fruit after four years, in due course he sends from abroad to collect his share. In all three versions the parable links the final dispossession of the vinedressers with the scribes and priests.[5] While the story could be imagined as happening anywhere in the middle east that supported the vine – from the Egyptian delta to Anatolia and Greece –, the parable strikingly repeats the theme of a man who tries, unsuccessfully, to supervise his material interests from afar.

Only Luke preserves the story of the unjust steward.[6] It poses complex ethical problems which it would have been more convenient to suppress and its survival gives it the authenticity which attaches to 'awkward' material. The answer to the puzzles may lie in the fact that the steward has taken interest (prohibited by the law of Moses) on behalf of his master, who as a pious Jew cannot object when he remits it. But the steward's ability to remit large debts on his own authority implies a considerable distance between his field of operation and the place where his lord is living.

If we suppose that Jesus and his mother had long been absent from Galilee, and had experienced the anxieties of those dependent on

---

[1] Mark 13, 33–34: JB.
[2] The gnostics, as well as those who practised the Hellenistic mysteries, were deeply concerned that the soul should not fall into the sleep of customary life.
[3] Matthew 25, 14–28.
[4] Luke 19, 12–27.
[5] Matthew 21, 33–46; Mark 12, 1–12; Luke 20, 9–19.
[6] Luke 16, 1–8.

agents for the supervision of their property, we are positing a perennial middle eastern situation. Many Lebanese today live abroad in
Africa or the Americas while retaining land and property in the
village at home. The parable of the talents bespeaks a familiarity with
a world in which investment of funds is a matter of understood concern.

Another figure to recur in the parables is the younger son, or late-
comer. It would be unwise to take this in isolation as establishing
Jesus's position in his family. The younger son plays an archetypal role
in the folk stories of many nations. In Jewish tradition, Benjamin, the
twelfth and last son of Jacob and Rachel, enjoys particular favour.
Popular champions such as Gideon, David and Judas Maccabaeus were
all younger brothers. But the central position, in the longest surviving
parable, not merely of a younger but of a wasteful and demanding
brother, could support the Catholic tradition that Jesus was Mary's
only child. This is also confirmed by the occasion on which his brothers seem to have thought him mad and 'set out to take charge of
him'.[1] It would have been unconventional to say the least, for younger
brothers so to treat their senior. But if Jesus were Joseph's youngest
son, by a second wife, returned late from abroad and engaging in practices that shocked public opinion, their reaction would be normal and
credible.

Before considering the important parable which describes the reconciliation of a disoriented young man with his father, it will be useful
to bear in mind the extremely short story, preserved by Matthew, in
which Jesus uses a surprising symbol. The story's brevity recalls the
Coptic texts recovered from the sands of Nag Hammadi in Upper
Egypt immediately after the Second World War.[2]

> Again, the kingdom of heaven is like a merchant looking for fine
> pearls; when he finds one of great value he goes and sells everything
> he owns and buys it.[3]

Here Jesus uses as his symbol of ultimate value the product of a
mollusc that inhabits a chaos of weeds and sewage; but even at its
purest the sea had none of the charm for the first century that it had for
Romantic poets or modern tourists. Yet its implications for the parable
of the prodigal son will become clear when we ponder whether Jesus
himself had sown the wild oats of youth. In the parable the younger
son begins by asking his father:

[1] Mark 3, 21: JB.
[2] *The Nag Hammadi Library*: James M. Robinson, general editor; New York, 1977.
[3] Matthew 13, 45–46: JB.

'Father, give me the share that is coming to me of the property.' So the father divided it between them. Not many days later the younger son packed together all he had and departed for a distant country and there lived it up till he had spent all his money. At that time the country underwent a severe famine which left him famished, too. So he signed up with one of the local citizens who sent him into his fields to feed the pigs. And he would have liked to join the pigs in eating their carob pods yet no one offered him a thing. Then waking up he said to himself: 'How many of my father's paid hands have more food than they need, while I am starving to death. I will clear off and go to my father and say: "Father, I have sinned against heaven and in your sight. I don't deserve still to be called your son. Treat me as one of your hands."' So he got up and went back to his father. His father saw him when he was still a long way off and was moved with pity. Running to the boy, he put his arms round his neck and kissed him. Then his son said, 'Father, I have sinned against heaven and in your sight. I don't deserve still to be called your son.' But the father said to his servants, 'Hurry, fetch the best robe and put it on him. Put a ring on his finger and sandals on his feet. Bring the wheat-fed calf and kill it. We are going to have a feast, since my son here was dead and has been raised to life, was lost and is found.' And they began to make merry. But the elder son was still out in the fields and on his way back, as he approached the house, he heard music and dancing. Calling one of the slaves, he asked what it was all about. 'Your brother has come,' he replied, 'and your father has killed the wheat-fed calf to celebrate his safe return.' The older brother was furious and refused to go in, but his father came out to reason with him. But he answered his father, 'Think of all the years I have slaved for you and never once gone against your orders yet never once have you offered me even a kid so I could make a party for my friends. But this son of yours, who's devoured your property with his whores, he comes back and you kill the best calf.' The father said, 'My son, you are always with me and all that is mine is yours. But it was right to feast and make merry, for your brother here was dead and has been raised, was lost and is found.'[1]

The story remains readily intelligible today though it is worth noting that under Jewish law the youth had no entitlement to a share of his father's property; this should have been conserved, rather, for the care of his parents in old age. The country to which he travels is unnamed, but is liable to famine and ignores the taboo on raising pigs. The story affects the reader on multiple levels. Superficially, heard for the first

[1] Luke 15, 11–32: DS.

time, it might be a coherent and moving folk-tale. Pondered for its ethical content, it illustrates the limiteless nature of God's forgiveness. Studied for what it reveals of the narrator's experience, it may unlock a major secret of the hidden years.

While absent from Mark and Matthew the parable of the prodigal son has one remarkable parallel in a piece of non-canonical Christian writing which stands out from most apocrypha. The Hymn of the Pearl, recognised as 'the first poem in all Syriac literature', occurs, as a detachable entity, in the *Acts of Thomas*.[1] It recalls the narrative structure of the parable.

The Ego who narrates the Hymn begins by describing his origin in his father's eastern palace. When still a child he is stripped of the purple robe that exactly fits his form and is sent, loaded with a burden that is at once heavy and light, to fetch from Egypt 'the one Pearl', sea-girt and guarded by a voracious serpent. His mission accomplished, the boy will be restored to royal state beside his brother.

The boy sets out with two guides on the road through Babylon. He is left alone once they reach Egypt, but makes one friend, a kindred soul who also derives from the east. Outwardly he apes the manners of the people while inwardly awaiting the moment to rob the serpent. But the Egyptians seem to know him and by luring him to partake of their food and drink they make him forget the Pearl.

Far off his parents are aware of what has happened and send a messenger to remind him of his mission and the gold-flecked robe which awaits his return.

> I remembered that I was a king's son,
> And my freeborn soul longed for its kind.
> I remembered the Pearl
> For which I had been sent down to Egypt,
> And I began to enchant
> The terrible and devouring serpent.
> I overcame him by naming
> The name of my Father upon him,
> The name of our next in rank,
> And the name of my mother, the queen of the East.
> I seized the Pearl,
> And turned to go back to my Father's house.

---

[1] The *Acts of Thomas* appear between pages 364 and 483 of *The Apocryphal New Testament*; tr. Montague Rhodes James, Oxford, 1924. These *Acts*, defined by James as a 'primary romance', share one characteristic with the far more important *Gospel of Thomas* (cf. Nag Hammadi Library): they assume that Thomas is the twin of Jesus. This may explain why the *Acts of Thomas* were thought a fitting reliquary for the Hymn.

Their filthy garment I shed,
And left it behind in Egypt.[1]

The Ego returns home where his father receives him at the gates of his kingdom.

Far older than the *Acts* in which it is lodged, the Hymn is often ascribed to a second-century heretic, Bardaisan. But it reads so much like an esoteric version of the prodigal son that it poses the question whether it may not derive from Jesus, however edited in special interests. As in the parables which Jesus explained to his disciples, the earthly details stand for cosmic ideas. The Hymn is as sun-centred as the Levant from which it derives. The kingdom of heaven is where the sun rises; the spiritual robe is the sun's colour; and the nobles adore the king in the manner of the children of the morning, the stars (or planets) that dance round the solar throne. The Pearl represents the ultimate quest, the gem-like treasure to be salvaged from the fouled fluidity of human life. The Nile (which Egyptians still refer to as *al-bahr*, the sea) stands for matter and darkness. The serpent is Tiamit, the chaos-monster. The luggage which the boy takes on his descent into Egypt stands for the gnosis, or knowledge of his true condition.

The Hymn, in short, mirrors the predicament of a soul beguiled from its purpose by the lures of matter. This echoes the parable and raises the possibility that disillusioning experiences may have prompted Jesus to the rediscovery of his true self. Such a suggestion pre-supposes, of course, that Jesus was fully a man and that, like other men, he reached his particular truth by a zigzag process, not in a trajectory of unwavering certitude.

If we accept that his longest parable has affinities with the Hymn, and that both speak of biographical experience, we can assume that in his yough Jesus had erred – or in the language of theology, 'sinned' – without hazarding too close a guess at what these errors were. The lives of later and better documented saints show how heavily almost imperceptible failing can weigh on the tender conscience; while, in the case of others, ascetic holiness may be a reaction to years of indulgence. 'The greatest saints,' Graham Greene has written, 'have been men with more than a normal capacity for evil, and the most vicious men have sometimes narrowly avoided sanctity.'[2] However this may be, the first action recorded of the adult Jesus shows him voluntarily undergoing a

---

[1] From the version of P. L. Travers in *Search, Journey on the Inner Path*; ed. Jean Sulzberger, New York, 1979. The Hymn, Mr. Travers points out, goes by other names, such as *Hymn of the Robe of Glory*, and *Hymn of the Soul*; but *Hymn of the Pearl* is the more accurate, 'for it is the Biblical pearl of great price that the hero is sent to retrieve'.

[2] *Frederick Rolfe: Edwardian Inferno* in *Collected Essays*.

rite designed to purge its practitioners from sin. His readiness to be submerged in the Jordan by a Judaean holy man gives little support to the later dogma that he was free from the normal movements of the flesh, then as now a prompter of guilt in most young males.[1]

---

[1] Or young people generally: the children who saw the Fatima Apparitions claimed that the Virgin informed them there were more people in hell for sins of the flesh than for any other form of wrongdoing.

CHAPTER SEVEN

His First Public Act

The baptism of Jesus may be taken as a fact of history if only because it would have been much simpler to omit from the record. From early days his acceptance of a rite designed to take away sin posed problems for the church. Our knowledge of its details must derive from what Jesus told one or more of his friends and shows the deep impression it made on him. Its importance to him, preceding as it did his decision to recruit disciples, must have been common knowledge. It was thus impossible to excise from the story of his mission.

The geographical setting the Baptist chose, the rite he performed, belong to a checkable world. For his own existence and career we have independent testimony in *The Antiquities of the Jews*, a twenty-volume history completed by Flavius Josephus in AD 93. This records the common Jewish belief that an Arabian king defeated Herod the Tetrarch in battle as punishment for his treatment of

> John, that was called the Baptist; for Herod slew him who was a good man and commanded the Jews who (already) exercised virtue, both as to righteousness towards one another, and piety towards God, to come together for baptism.[1]

Josephus wrote his monumental work, our major source for much Jewish history, after the Romans had suppressed a nationalist revolt and sacked Jerusalem. Despite his own collaboration with the Romans he aimed by his writings to increase understanding of his people. He tended to spiritualise, or make less farouche, movements of Jewish revival. He was nevertheless loathed by Jews and his well-intentioned writings survive thanks to Christian copyists, who were not above fudging where matters affecting their doctrines were involved: a paragraph referring to Jesus has become so reverential that it raises the question of why Josephus, if he felt so impressed, had not become a follower. But in the case of the Baptist there are no signs of major editing and the passage confirms the background to the gospel stories.

The Jordan, unlike some other place names in the texts, raises no problem. A narrow, sedgy and sometimes muddy river, it carried the

[1] Book XVIII, Chapter V, Section 2.

excess water of the Sea of Galilee south to the Dead Sea. Its valley was a deep and often sombre gash in the earth's crust.

The elements in John's rite were as old as near eastern religion. The pharaohs had undergone a ceremony of baptism which was seen as a royal renewal corresponding to the sun's daily submergence in the sea. The mystery cults of the Roman empire also used immersion. According to Tertullian, men were baptised at Eleusis. He adds that the font was also used by the initiates of Isis and Mithras. 'Among the ancients, anyone who had stained himself with homicide sought waters that could purge him of his guilt.' The Essenes, too, practised a baptism ritual while today, according to the latest edition of the New Standard Jewish Encyclopaedia, 'an essential part of the rite of conversion to Judaism in the case of either sex is immersion in water to the accompaniment of special prayers'. John gave his own colouring to the rite. Like many of his contemporaries, he felt that the world was approaching a dramatic climax and men should meet this purged from guilt; his method of purgation was cheaper and purer than the rituals of animal sacrifice normally used. The crowds who flocked to the Jordan must have appreciated the economy of the rite but their failure to offer an animal or bird at the Jerusalem altar will have made the Baptist less than popular with the priests.

The modern European seeks the sea, with other aspects of rugged nature, for his annual vacation; he looks upon water (unless fouled by industrial pollution) as the symbol of purity. Not so the ancients. They regarded the sea as a symbol of primeval chaos and their mental picture of the cosmos (which Jesus shared) was of *terra firma* surrounded by, or balanced on, watery confusion. The earth resembled, indeed, the Ego of Freudian terminology as it rose from the threatening Id of ocean. While naturally water was used in everyday life for cleansing, for the participants in the mysteries it stood for their subsidence into an element representing death prior to their emergence from it reborn. Those burdened with guilt flocked to baptism. But for someone untainted by sin to accept this expiation was as inappropriate as it would be for a healthy person to attend a clinic and request penicillin.

Yet all four gospels regard the baptism of Jesus as the first act in his public career. Each version of what happened differs slightly from the next but it is clear that he underwent the ritual alone and with no disciple present; the Baptist himself, later evidence confirms, reached no particular conclusion as a result of the event.[1]

Peter, Mark's source, had yet to meet Jesus at the time of the baptism:

---

[1] Cf. Matthew 11, 2–6 and Luke 7, 18–23.

No sooner had he come up out of the water than he saw the heavens
torn apart and the Spirit, like a dove, descending on him. And a
voice came from heaven, 'You are my Son, the Beloved; my favour
rests on you.'[1]

Matthew's modification of Mark's account shows that he was aware
of problems:

John tried to dissuade him. 'It is I who need baptism from you,' he
said, 'and yet you come to me!' . . . As soon as Jesus was baptised he
came up from the water, and suddenly the heavens opened and he
saw the Spirit of God descending like a dove and coming down on
him. And a voice spoke from heaven, 'This is my Son, the Beloved;
my favour rests on him.'[2]

The personal nature of the experience, which suggested to Jesus the
descent of a bird, is preserved; but the text leaves it open whether or
not the Voice was heard by others.

Luke, the fabulising Hellenist, changes the story in two ways. He
pushes the ritual itself off-stage, into the phrase 'after his own
baptism', while depicting the subsequent occurrences as concrete and
external:

Now when all the people had been baptised and while Jesus after his
own baptism was at prayer, heaven opened and the Holy Spirit descended on him in bodily shape, like a dove. And a voice came from
heaven, 'You are my Son, the Beloved; my favour rests on you.'[3]

John attributes his account to the Baptist, who reduces Luke's bodily
descent of the dove to a simile:

I saw the Spirit coming down on him from heaven like a dove and
resting on him. I did not know him myself, but he who sent me to
baptise with water had said to me, 'The man on whom you see the
Spirit come down and rest is the one who is going to baptise with the
Holy Spirit.'[4]

John has already, in his first chapter, stressed the Baptist's inferiority
to Jesus. This polemical approach was probably due to the persistence
at Ephesus (with which the author of the fourth gospel is traditionally
linked) of disciples of the Baptist who refused to accept Jesus as their
master's superior. Be that as it may, John's account of the events by the
Jordan could hardly have come from the Baptist, who was arrested
soon afterwards for offending Herod the Tetrarch and from his

[1] Mark 1, 9–11: JB.
[2] Matthew 3, 13–17: JB.
[3] Luke 3, 21–22: JB.
[4] John 1, 32–33: JB.

dungeon made inquiries about the identity of Jesus. He was put to death by Herod before he could see Jesus again. But John's account is interesting for its failure to confirm the family relationship worked out so carefully by Luke in his infancy chapters.

Jesus must have discussed his baptismal experience with several of his disciples, but Peter was plainly the most important. Peter's recollection, passed on to his amanuensis, Mark, provides the relatively clear outline which underlies the three other versions. Jesus, it is evident, had walked from his lodgings unaccompanied, unremarked, to the stretch of water south of the lake where the Baptist stood. With other penitents he had waded into the river and waited his turn to be doused by John. At which point an experience sudden as migraine overwhelmed him.

Six centuries later the prophetic career of Muhammad was to open with a similarly momentous experience. In his case, it was preceded by a period of fasting and meditation in a mountain cave and left him trembling and afraid. His experience, like that of Jesus, involved a vision and a communication. In the case of Muhammad, this was a command to recite in the name of his Lord. The fact that two versions of what he saw survive – in one, a vision of God himself, in a second of Gabriel[1] – show how such overwhelming experiences tend afterwards to blur like much-handled wax. Muhammad's experience comes to us through third parties transmitting accounts several generations later. The approximation of all such accounts to the original experience is necessarily rough.

The experience happened to Jesus when he had come from afar after, we may assume, a long period of questioning and spiritual malaise. The importance given to it in all four accounts proves its subjective force. If the original awe inevitably fades from the accounts of narrators, these retain the proclamation, by the Voice, of an intimate bond between itself and Jesus.

This unique experience has no need to be interpreted in terms of scriptural tradition. Although Yahweh supposedly sent ravens to feed one prophet,[2] he did not customarily manifest himself in descending birds. Doves, in any case, were sacred to the pagan goddess of love, whether known as Aphrodite or Astarte. Yahweh had preferred to appear in more violent symbols: the burning bush, the plagues which he sent upon Egypt, the flame-pillar and dust-pillar which led the Israelites on the march, or the mysterious night-wrestler who fought

[1] W. Montgomery Watt: op.cit., p. 42, discussing an account of two visions in the Koran: 'The usual exegesis of this by Muslims is that these were visions of Gabriel; but there are grounds for thinking that Muhammad originally interpreted these as visions of God Himself.'
[2] 1 Kings 17, 6.

with Jacob. The identification of the visionary bird may derive from Jesus himself, or later tradition. Mystical apparitions are in any case probably too swift for ornithological exactitude.[1]

For what Jesus thought he saw, Egypt provides better guidance than a bird-book. Rê, the sun god, maintained the same parental closeness to the Ptolemies and the Caesars as he had to the pharaohs of the Old Kingdom or to Akhnaton, whose cult of the sun-disc lowering hands of blessing on the royal family was a restatement of the perennial religion. When Rê held his beloved, the pharaoh, to his bosom, he did so in the guise of Horus, whose commonest symbol was the hawk, the bird that seemed to fly closest to the sun and to descend from it with the greatest rush. The adoption, in a baptismal rite, of a mortal by a deity posed no major problem to Egyptians. They conceived of the divine power as multi-faceted, multisexual, a cosmic diamond, not a single cosmic despot, transcendent and male. This Egyptian atttitude was widely shared by a syncretist middle east. And by the first century the sun had become chief figure in most religious cults.

Luke's dating of the baptism poses minor problems compared with those raised by his dating of the nativity.[2] If around AD 28 Jesus had returned to northern Palestine, his soul reflecting perceptions akin to those in the Hymn of the Pearl, the experience by the Jordan must have come with energising impact. Its constituents – the apparent opening of heaven, the descent of the bird, the Voice declaring him 'my Son, the Beloved' – constituted the spiritual equivalent of a carnal adventure's festal robe and wheat-fed calf. Jesus had brought the gnosis symbolised by the Pearl from the Egyptian delta and was now to share it with those still sleeping.

[1] In this writer's experience, few middle easterners distinguish geese from swans and colour differentiation has hardly developed from Roman times.
[2] Luke sets the start of the ministry in the fifteenth regnal year of Tiberius. According to the Roman system, Tiberius started his fifteenth year on 19 August AD 28; but Luke may have gone by the Syrian system, in which case the key year would have started in the autumn of AD 27.

CHAPTER EIGHT

The Temptation And The Tempter

The gospel accounts appear to diverge sharply once Jesus leaves the Jordan valley. The first three depict him leaving civilisation for the desert, there to undergo the spiritual distress which is a known consequence of mystical exaltation. But John has no dark night of the soul. Jesus enlists a group of disciples and then attends a village wedding before proceeding to Jerusalem for the passover and his first clash with institutional religion.

Which account are we to credit? What explains the apparent divergence between the narrative?

The nature and purpose of the fourth gospel provide an answer. The man whose experience is its prime source, who wrote in awareness of what his predecessors had written, stresses the events which he knew to be important. The theory that his gospel was an answer, a conscious corrective, is confirmed by the discovery in the depository for used books attached to Cairo's oldest synagogue. An Arabic-language version of a second-century attempt to harmonise the four gospels, gives, in its preamble, a descriptive epithet to each of the gospels. John's is named as *muib*, 'he who gives a reply'.[1] We may justifiably picture the author (without forgetting his reliance on secretaries and subjection to editors) as an old man putting right what he sees as incorrect in the first three gospels. Where he concurs with them, or has nothing to add from his own experience, he is silent. The fact, for example, that John reports none of the parables does not mean that he questions Jesus's use of the parable form or the broad accuracy of the versions recorded by his predecessors. His failure, therefore, to mention the desert ordeal does not imply that he doubted that Jesus temporarily withdrew from human society and was tempted. But for John, the temptation came immediately before the most important experience in his own life – his first encounter with Jesus. He had no quarrel with the versions of the temptation deriving from what Peter heard from Jesus; John himself was to explain their import throughout his gospel.

Immediately after the baptism, as Mark tells us, 'the Spirit drove

[1] Cf. Paul E. Kahle: *The Cairo Geniza*, Oxford, 1959: p.300.

him out into the wilderness and he remained there for forty days, and was tempted by Satan. He was with the wild beasts, and the angels looked after him.'[1] Mark places this withdrawal immediately before the arrest of the Baptist. Forty days was a conventional figure for a longish time and the duration of the ordeal is imprecise. Jesus was still unknown and unaccompanied.

The brevity of Mark's account probably reflects his informant, the literal-minded, unimaginative Peter, at that time preoccupied with domestic problems. Mark says nothing of the content of the temptations, yet the topic was such as to fascinate first-century man. Matthew and Luke provide amplifications from a shared source, which may be the result of inquiries from some more inquisitive disciple, or conceivably someone's imagination. Whatever the provenance of this supplementary material, Matthew and Luke use it in characteristic ways.

Matthew names the tempter as the Greek *diabolus*, not the Aramaic Satan. Jesus, in this version, fasted, which is different from saying that he ate nothing. The first temptation is nonetheless prompted by physical hunger. 'If you are the Son of God' – the tempter takes up the title proclaimed by the Voice – 'command these stones to become loaves.' In the second temptation the *diabolus* takes Jesus to the parapet of Herod's temple and urges him to perform a wonder and throw himself down. In the third, the tempter takes him to a high mountain where in a flash he displays the kingdoms of the world and offers their power and glory to Jesus in return for worship. Matthew, who marks each temptation with the swopping of scriptural texts, ends the ordeal with his return to Galilee, a journey which agrees with the otherwise silent John.

Luke, who delights in literal miracles, has Jesus eating no food whatsoever for forty days. The first temptation is the same as in Matthew but the next two are implausibly reversed. Luke has Jesus first tempted with world-rule and then with the prospect of applause for a trick of downward levitation (if that is not a verbal contradiction). Luke ends with the intriguing sentence that the devil left him, to return at the appointed time.

Since the ordeal follows so swiftly the revelation by the Jordan, the first question is the identity of the tempter.

The problem of the origin of evil preoccupied many in the first-century Levant. Neither Judaism nor any other monotheistic philosophy has found it easy to reconcile the cosmic rule of a unique and beneficent creator with the introduction into his cosmos of evident evil. The notion of a devil – 'he who hinders' in its Semitic form, 'he who slanders' in its Greek – reduced the stature of the antagonist but did not explain why a malign element should exist at all.

[1] Mark 1, 12–13: JB.

The tempter reveals himself to Jesus by what he offers and by what he controls. He envisages the production of food through a spell. He proposes wonders. He offers political power. The god who was believed to have massacred the firstborn of the Egyptians manifested just such powers. He had sustained the children of Israel on manna. He had parted the Red Sea, made the sun stand still for Joshua, and, through Elisha, made an iron axe swim. Political power was certainly within his competence and at the popular level the messiah was foreseen as a conqueror destined to evict the foreigner from Israel and establish an empire.

When Jesus rejects these temptations he is taking his first step as a revolutionary inside his society. The Voice above the Jordan belonged less to Yahweh than to the beneficent father portrayed in the Aton cult as a disc with descending hands: a god whom the revolutionary pharaoh had hymned for his goodness to all men and concern for all creatures. The tempter is close in spirit to the antagonist of Horus, the Set who reigning in desolate places was identified in the Egyptian mind with Asia. Yet pharaonic religion, like the Hindu, was not tripped up by the existence of a destructive god, since destruction formed part of cosmic function. Set seemed evil to human sufferers but remained nonetheless the brother of Horus. Only when a supreme god becomes a sole god does his involvement with evil become an obsessive problem.

An example from Hebrew history illustrates the problem. The ancient Israelites had been taught that it was sinful to conduct a census of the people. Yet while planning the temple David numbered his people. The spirit which prompted the king to commit a sin (and a sin destined to cause many deaths by epidemic) is described in alternative terms by two Old Testament books. Samuel attributes David's ill-fated inspiration to Yahweh himself:

> The anger of Yahweh once again blazed out against the Israelites and he incited David against them. 'Go,' he said, 'take a census of Israel and Judah.'[1]

Chronicles, a later version, attributes David's decision to the devil.

> Satan rose against Israel and incited David to take a census of the Israelites.[2]

Sigmund Freud, in his ingenious *Moses and Monotheism*, explained the conundrum at the heart of the Jewish tradition by the survival, side by side, of two contrasted visions of deity. Moses had been an Egypt-

---

[1] 2 Samuel 24, 1: JB.
[2] 1 Chronicles 21, 1: JB.

ian adherent to Akhnaton's universalist religion. After the priests of Amen-Rê restored the older cult, Moses imparted the new faith to the Hebrews, a nomadic tribe, whom he led into exile. The non-territorial tribe of Levi, Freud suggested, descended from a body of Egyptian Atonists who joined the Exodus. Even more daringly, the apostle of the Oedipus Complex proposed that the Old Testament concealed a great secret: his adopted people murdered Moses under the influence of an Asian deity of war and violence, the Yahweh whose cult they encountered somewhere between Egypt and Canaan.

However we rate this theory, the Old Testament authors sensed a problem which later ecclesiastics were virtually to shelve. But while Christian orthodoxy was to affirm that the god of love and mercy preached by Jesus was the same cosmic force as had incited Joshua to genocide in Canaan or used Elisha to transfer leprosy from one man to another,[1] on the popular level the Yahwist elements inside Christianity have been largely suppressed;[2] the man in the street who believes in God believes in a benevolent sky-figure. Since Persian times much the same suppression had taken place in the Levant, among the Jews as among their neighbours. In the temptations Jesus rejected the Yahwist aspects of a syncretic deity.

If his baptism was the most ecstatic event in his life, the ordeal in the desert was the most decisive. On the first occasion the Voice had assured him he was the beloved of God. His days of mental turmoil convinced him who this god was not.

On the fringe of the great desert which stretches south from the Syrian steppe through the Arabian plateau to the total aridity of the Empty Quarter, Yahweh had endeavoured to assert his claims. The tempter in the Judaean wilderness represented the counter-attack of an aspect of deity Jesus had probably long rejected but that remained latent in his unconscious. The three temptations were linked by power: the power to solve man's economic problems; the power to impress by prodigies or magic; above all, the power to rule men. If these temptations had emanated from the kind of horned demon beloved by medieval painters, they would have been trivial. But if they came from the god who played a central role in the traditions of his people, Jesus set his feet on the path to martyrdom in rejecting them one by one.

---

[1] 2 Kings 5, 10–14 & 27.
[2] Except among ecclesiastics in time of war or campaigns of moral renovation.

CHAPTER NINE

A Nucleus Of Followers

After these two experiences Jesus becomes involved, for the first time, with named individuals of his own generation. The friendships of his youth are unknown to us but it is unlikely they were formed in Galilee. There he appears what the Coptic texts were to call him, *ho allogenês*, 'the foreigner'; as he says of himself, unlike the foxes who have lairs or the birds that have nests, he has no settled abode. And now there is a significant swerve to the story. Jesus is no longer the source of the records. Henceforth their material and arrangement derive from reports or rumours; these have in turn been edited or, in some cases, interwoven with fantasy and mythical pattern-making.

The first three gospels are in basic agreement – or follow Mark – on the consitution of the initial group. Mark's source, Peter, would not easily have forgotten the circumstances of his own recruitment. But when later the first nucleus becomes a band of twelve, we have no way of knowing whether this was a fact, or an Old Testament stencil imposed on fact, to repeat the traditional number of the Hebrew tribes. No list of the twelve is precisely identical with another.

In Mark's account, Jesus is strolling by the lakeside when he sees two brothers, Simon and Andrew, casting nets into the water. Jesus summons them to be fishers of men and they at once obey.[1]

Matthew follows Mark with minimal changes.[2] His reference to 'Simon called Peter' makes it possible that 'Petros' was Simon's original Greek nickname; his brother, too, had a Greek name and John, in his first reference to him, calls him 'Simon Peter'.[3] (In the same tradition, twentieth-century Lebanon abounds in names like Clovis, Henri or Camille.) The next two recruits are James and John, the sons of Zebedee.

Luke, while naming the same initial four, conflates details from other occasions. For example, Jesus borrows Simon's boat to address a crowd on the shore, which would imply that he had already started preaching; the complaining Simon has a miraculous run of luck after a

[1] Mark 1, 16–20.
[2] Matthew 4, 18–22.
[3] John 1, 40.

night of profitless fishing. The sons of Zebedee are business partners of Simon and Andrew and this reminds us of how earlier Luke had made Jesus John the Baptist's cousin.[1]

A surprise awaits us when we turn to John. His initial recruits are not mariners, fishing as in Mark/Matthew, or cleaning their boats as in Luke, and the scene is different. The Baptist is standing at his customary place by the river when Jesus passes.[2] John points him out with such reverence that 'two of his disciples' at once pursue the stranger. Their movements have something of the haste of a pick-up. Jesus stops in his tracks.

'What do you want?'

The pair ask where he lives.

'Come and see.'

John's two disciples go and see where he lives and stay with him for the rest of the day. 'It was about the tenth hour': i.e. about 4 pm.

The clarity of the scene, the precision as to time, suggest that in the Baptist's susceptible disciple we have the unnamed source of the gospel. The second disciple, Andrew, is named. And next morning Andrew tells his brother, Simon Peter, that they have found a guru superior to John. Peter is taken to meet Jesus and become a disciple. The conversion of these three is followed by that of Philip, who is a fellow-townsman of Andrew and Peter. Philip then introduces Nathanael, the fifth disciple. A later passage links him with Cana.[3]

The introduction of Peter and Nathanael, like all the fourth gospel, has been through multiple stages of revision and censorship which must account for some of the detail. Andrew does not, of course, refer to a guru. That is my gloss for his alleged statement, improbable in the context, '"We have found the Messiah!" which means, the Christ.' Much of the talk between Philip and Nathanael, then between Nathanael and Jesus, reflects later theology.

'The one Moses wrote of in the Law, and the prophets too, we've found: Jesus son of Joseph, from Nazareth.'

'Can anything good,' Nathanael replied, 'come from Nazareth?'

'Come and see for yourself,' said Philip.

Jesus saw Nathanael approaching and commented: 'There goes a genuine Israelite, one without trickery.'

'How do you know me?' asked Nathanael.

'Before Philip called you,' said Jesus, 'I saw you under the fig-tree.'

[1] Luke 5, 1–11.
[2] Although the passage (John 1, 35–39) begins 'On the following day', like many temporary connections in the gospels this is not necessarily factual and need not controvert the picture of Jesus as then on his way back from the desert.
[3] John 21, 2.

Nathanael answered, 'Rabbi, you are the Son of God, you are the king of Israel.'

Jesus replied, 'Because I told you that I saw you under the fig-tree, you believe? Truly I tell you: you will see the sky opened up and the angels of God ascending and descending above me.'[1]

It is very unlikely that Philip identified Jesus with the Messiah on such brief acquaintance, or that Nathanael should have proclaimed him the Son of God. He had manifested none of the traits of the expected messiah while the works attributed to Moses predict no such figure, who is mentioned only in some of the later prophets. It is also improbable that one instance of clairvoyance would have convinced Nathanael, still an orthodox Jew, that Jesus was a divine man and not a wonder-worker. The editors of John's text have reworked the passage to fit more developed doctrines. While 'the Son of God' does echo the words of the Voice, Jesus had not yet had time to describe his baptism to others. If, in John's original version, Philip referred to Moses, it was more likely to draw parallels between Jesus (who may already have acquired a reputation as a healer) and the lawgiver; a later disciple was to be impressed by two such parallels: Jesus had lived in Egypt like Moses and like Moses had learnt the wisdom of the Egyptians.[2] The most interesting distortion is probably the reference to the angels. John was long suspected of gnostic leanings and his editors may here have doctored a passage more compromising than the famous Prologue. For the gnostics were obsessed with the problem of how the universe had come to be. They postulated, and often named, a series of *archons,* or cosmic rulers, descending in a spiral of diminishing power from the supreme God with whom Jesus now felt himself in intimate touch.

But what gives this episode in John its unassailable interest is its introduction of the unnamed disciple. For he, with Peter, is to emerge as one of the two subsidiary characters in the New Testament to exhibit recognisable personality. They do so in two important ways: in their contributions to the story of Jesus, and in their actions. Peter's reflections on Jesus, as mediated through Mark, are less important than his actions, since his understanding of what Jesus intended seems frequently shallow. John shows a more even balance between an actor in the drama and a mind interpreting a series of enigmatic sayings and events.

[1] John 1, 45–51: DS.

[2] As we see in greater detail later, the first martyr, Stephen, develops in his interrupted *Apologia* (*Acts of the Apostles* 7) a comparison between Jesus and Moses who was taught all the wisdom of the Egyptians and became a man with power both in his speech and actions. If Stephen had had time to complete his defence, he might have confirmed Freud in his supposition that Moses, like Jesus, was a victim of his people.

In this early passage the unnamed disciple's abrupt shift of allegiance from the Baptist to Jesus fits with a perennial religious type. He
prefigures the Francis of Assisi who abandons wealth on an impulse,
the young Oxonian who tries a new church each Sunday or the Califor-
nian who moves from cult to cult. His ignorance of where Jesus lives
suggests that he was himself a stranger to Galilee, for the men of the
province would have known every move of one who had either recently
returned to Nazareth from abroad (as I surmise was the case) or who
had lived there all his life. The young man's familiarity, towards the
end of the drama, with the High Priest's household suggests a connection not merely with Jerusalem but with its dominant caste. His intellectual culture, as revealed in his gospel, manifests the synthesis
between Judaism and Hellenism best exemplified in the writings of
Philo of Alexandria; the term Logos used in the prologue to the fourth
gospel acquired its theological meaning in the conscious effort to link
Hebrew monotheism with classical philosophy. The same syncretic
culture was to be found to greater or less degree in all the Greek cities
of western Asia, and notably in Ephesus. The obstinate tradition
which was to link Mary to Ephesus and to the 'beloved disciple' has
external evidence to support it. This evidence also sheds light on the
most mysterious figure in the entourage of Jesus.

The evidence relating to John derives from the fourth-century
church historian Eusebius. He tells how one of the few early authorities on the apostolic age, Papias from what is now Pamukkale in
south-west Turkey, had diligently sought out anyone who had known
contemporaries of Jesus to ask them for quotations from 'Andrew,
Peter, Philip, Thomas, James, John, Matthew or any other of the disciples and also from those other disciples, Aristion and John the
Presbyter'. Philip, one of this list, had traditionally lived in the same
city as Papias. Eusebius believed that Papias thus confirmed a tradition known to him, that two separate Johns had lived in Ephesus.[1]
For the city boasted two tombs, each ascribed to 'John'. Eusebius
claims that the John who had written the gospel and had been the
beloved disciple had returned to Asia Minor after the death of
Domitian[2] and had administered churches on the mainland. This
John, again according to Eusebius, survived into the reign of Trajan.[3]
Clement of Alexandria, the second-century convert from Hellenistic
paganism, contributes further evidence in his treatise *What Rich Man
Is To Be Saved?* This argues that not all rich men fall under Jesus's

[1] Eusebius, *Ecclesiastical History*, III, XXXIX.
[2] This unsavoury emperor was stabbed in his bedroom by a freedman named
Stephanus on 18 September AD 96. John's traditional place of exile was the island of
Patmos.
[3] AD 98–117.

general condemnation.¹ Clement describes an aged John installing new bishops in what is now Aegean Turkey. One particular incident has psychological relevance to the authorship of the fourth gospel.

On one visit, Clement tells us, the old man was so captivated by a youth of attractive appearance and ardent mind that he commended the young man to the special care of the local ecclesiastic. But after John had returned to Ephesus, the young man fell into the company of rascals and, from being a promising Christian, became the first-century equivalent of a gang-leader. A single expedition for plunder sufficed to make the young man surpass his peers in blood-lust and cruelty. John was totally unaware of these developments and when he next visited the town he asked for 'the return of his deposit'. The cleric took John to mean a sum of money and was astounded to learn that it was the ruffian he wanted. When he realised what had befallen his protégé, John left at once for the scrub country to the east and en route was taken prisoner by the bandit's guard. Clement gives his tale a happy ending. The youth repented of his violent life: 'so furnishing striking evidence of regeneration, a trophy of a visible resurrection.'²

The acceptance of the author of the fourth gospel as the favourite of Jesus demands a qualifying word. The self-conferred phrase persuaded the playwright Christopher Marlowe that Jesus felt for John what Socrates had professed for Phaedo, the converted slave. But Jesus himself is nowhere quoted as saying that he preferred one of his disciples to the others or that his male followers meant more to him than the many women, such as Mary of Magdala, who apparently followed him from place to place. The author of the fourth gospel is the only source to this claim to pre-eminence. The claim, which the other three gospels pass over in silence, is understandable from an old man who had outlived his contemporaries and whose fame in the community depended upon a long distant association with one revered as more than a prophet.³ Clement's description of the old man's susceptibility to an attractive, if dangerous youth, fits the emotional bias of his gospel better than the wrangling about priority in the Kingdom which preoccupies John, son of Zebedee, thought by some to be the author of the gospel.⁴ This earthier John, according to an early tradition, was

¹ Clement was honoured as a saint of the universal Church until his somewhat capricious decanonisation by Pope Benedict XIV in the mid-eighteenth century.
² Eusebius, op.cit., III, XXIII.
³ Mark 10, 35–45 has James and John, the sons of Zebedee, demand on their own behalf the right to sit on each side of Jesus in his kingdom; Matthew 20, 20–28 has their mother requesting this privilege on their behalf.
⁴ Although this study adopts the generally accepted view that the fourth Gospel dates from somewhere in the last ten years of the first century AD, strong arguments have recently been adduced for its composition being at least as early as any of the other gospels. Especially notable is J. A. T. Robinson's *Redating The New Testament*,

martyred along with his brother James in the 40s of the first century.[1]

London, 1976: he concludes (p.307) that the first edition of the fourth Gospel was written in Asia Minor between AD 50–55 and received its final form, with the addition of the prologue and epilogue, before AD 70. Without accepting Robinson's belief that the gospel-writer, the beloved disciple, and John the son of Zebedee were one and the same, an early dating would only serve to strengthen our belief in the value of John's Gospel for recovering the historical truth about Jesus.

[1] Philip of Side (AD 430) and George Hamartolus (ninth century) cite Papias as the source for the story that the Jews killed the sons of Zebedee in the 40s. Two martyrologies, from Carthage and Edessa, preserve the same tradition. Cf. *The Gospel According to John*: Raymond E. Brown, Anchor Bible.

CHAPTER TEN

What Was The Programme?

The purpose for which disciples of temperaments varying from the prosaic to the ecstatic attached themselves to Jesus is swaddled in an ambiguity which the four gospel-writers cannot unwrap. While all agree that the life and death of Jesus constituted a supreme event in human history, their interpretations of his programme significantly differ. One extreme is to be found in the account that derives from Simon Peter, the married Galilean fisherman who traditionally instructed Mark, and another in the contribution from the disciple who claimed priority in Jesus's affections.

The changing attitude of Jesus himself to his mission and hesitations about how he should attempt to fulfill it fostered ambiguity. Hesitations, even doubts, are normal parts of the dialectical development common to artists, thinkers and religious innovators. The life of Muhammad, his most challenging successor, illustrated how a process of development affects the purveyor of a revelation. The marked contrast in style and content between Muhammad's utterances at Mecca and those at Medina after he had organised a community has led to a division of the Koran into chapters based on their place of revelation. This division in its turn implies a time sequence, since Muhammad concentrated the first phase of his mission on Mecca and the second and last on Medina.

Those who heard Jesus and diffused his message or his reputation are a second source of ambiguity. To the majority of his contemporaries, indifferent, hostile, impressed but uncommitted, Jesus probably seemed a standard magician.[1] His methods of therapy, the adjuncts to faith on which he relied, such as mud or spittle, the verbal formulae he used undeniably belong to the age and place in which he lived. Sharing the general view that the indwelling of noxious spirits caused disease, he exorcised these to effect his cures. Those whom he healed acclaimed him as a thaumaturge. His enemies saw a trickster, a charlatan, a boaster. Only his intimates saw an individual with a sense of mission, and these differed in their notions of what this mission was.

When Mark worked the sayings he had collected from Peter and

[1] Cf. Morton Smith: *Jesus the Magician*, New York, 1978.

others into a narrative he created a portrait and plot which convinced Albert Schweitzer. The theologian from Alsace who was also a physician and exponent of Bach concluded his quest for the historical Jesus: 'Modern historical theology with its three-quarter scepticism is left at last with only a torn and tattered Gospel of Mark in its hands.'[1] Schweitzer wrote before the popularisation of modern psychology, before the papyri from Egypt had been properly edited and long before the Essene library at Qumran or the Gnostic library at Nag Hammadi had been discovered. From the hints of motivation and mission in Mark, Schweitzer abstracted his portrait of a pious Jew who becomes aware at baptism that he is the expected messiah. This destiny subsumes a double belief: that the Kingdom of God is about to be realised on earth, and that Jesus himself is to inaugurate its triumph. It becomes the secret which explains and destroys his life. He optimistically despatches seventy apostles whom he expects not to see again in the present age, as his coming in glory – or 'Parousia', in the theologians' term – will have meanwhile intervened. But the persecutions he predicts, and the dramatic appearance of the Kingdom which they are supposed to herald, do not happen. 'The whole history of "Christianity" down to the present day, that is to say, the real inner history of it, is based on the delay of the Parousia, the non-occurrence of the Parousia, the abandonment of eschatology, the progress and completion of the "de-eschatologising" of religion which has been connected therewith.'

Schweitzer's Jesus, tormented by the wish to escape people, crosses and recrosses the Jordan; disappears to the north; appears to some of his disciples transfigured on a mountain top near Caesarea Philippi; but increasingly realises that if he is to reappear in glory, he must first be snatched away – in other words, be put to death. The pivot of the Schweitzer gospel is the impetuous Peter's recognition of Jesus as the messiah and his disclosure of the secret to the twelve, including Judas. Jesus decides to go to Jerusalem, to suffer death there at the hands of the authorities. 'Towards Passover, therefore, Jesus sets out for Jerusalem, solely in order to die there.' When he speaks of dying for 'many', Schweitzer interprets these as Jews destined for the Kingdom.

At midday of the same day – it was the 14th Nisan, and in the evening the Paschal lamb would be eaten – Jesus cried aloud and expired. He had chosen to remain fully conscious to the last.

It is difficult to see how this deluded messiah, however resolute, could have had lasting importance. The 'end of the world' predictions,

[1] *Von Reimarus zu Wrede*: Albert Schweitzer, 1906; first English ed., *The Quest of the Historical Jesus*, 1910; tr. W. Montgomery. Quotations are from 3rd edition, London, 1973.

central to Schweitzer's view of his message, were provincial, ethnocentric – and unfulfilled. To someone who did not share the beliefs of the Jews about themselves, the concept of a young man dying to precipitate Israel's global triumph would be no more than historically curious. Few Jews were to recognise the figure on the cross as the expected deliverer.

Does Matthew extract a more credible programme? He wrote when Jerusalem had been laid waste and its religious authorities killed or scattered. A Christian church was preparing to substitute its authority for that of the synagogue. His gospel remoulds Mark in an ecclesiastical interest. While scolding the Jews, he insists that their tradition was central to the human drama and that Jesus completed it.

Luke, too, reworked Mark, but in his case for the Hellenistic world which he had helped Paul to evangelise. His agreeable style used literary devices popular with writers of the day.

Only John breaks radically with Mark. He identifies the Jesus he had loved with a philosophical construct, the Logos, or Word, which he sets in a cosmic struggle between light and darkness.

The ambiguities which derive from the changing moods of Jesus and from the contrasted interpretations of those who came within his orbit are in a sense accidental. But the contrast between the public and private teaching of Jesus, between what he said to the crowds and what he confided to such intimates as John, produces ambiguities of a profounder sort. Stylistically the contrast is marked by the difference between stark, sometimes puzzling utterances in the synoptics and the dithyrambic passages worked out by John. (The repetitiveness of the latter must, of course, owe something to the circumstances of an old man remembering.) If we take John seriously, if we accept that his gospel does in some measure project a truthful memory rather than an imagination, we are forced to assume that Jesus was far more than Schweitzer's obedient victim of a messianic delusion. If we open our minds to this possibility, we find that even the first three gospels conceal hints that justify the fourth. The synoptics cannot, for example, suppress the alarm which his more heterodox teaching inspired in his own family and their Galilean neighbours. This confirms Clement's argument (to be discussed again in Chapter XV, where it has particular relevance) that Jesus practised what theologians call reserve, the withholding of certain truths from those not ready for them. Even the fourth gospel probably clips the full boldness of Jesus's thought. Even if John had not censored some things himself, second-century editors whose chief opponents belonged to the gnostic movement will have scrutinised each phrase.

An interesting fourth-century tradition claims that John employed as amanuensis the man whom second-century orthodoxy came most to fear: Marcion, the son of a bishop from the Black Sea coast.[1] The best textual critic that early Christianity produced, Marcion was not a gnostic in the usual sense of that always elastic term. Yet he could not bring himself to identify the Old Testament's Yahweh, a god of justice and vengeance, with the god of mercy and love preached by Jesus.[2] Apart from his possible link with John, Marcion was the first man to edit a volume of Christian scripture to set against the scripture of the Jews. This primitive New Testament consisted of Luke (minus the infancy chapters and genealogy) and the major letters of Paul (minus some passages which he regarded as insertions).[3] When Rome rejected his standpoint, Marcion founded his own church and this for some decades threatened the supremacy of the orthodox church. Quotations from Marcion which survive in the works of his enemies illustrate the radical difference between his understanding of Jesus's mission and the official version.

In the 'special material' of Matthew – that is, material not found in Mark or the other gospels – Jesus is made to declare:

> Don't think that I came to abolish the Law or the prophets. I did not come to abolish but to fulfill. For I tell you truly: until the sky and the earth pass away, not one iota, not one accent shall pass from the Law till all is achieved.[4]

Even stranger is another passage where the teaching authority of the scribes and Pharisees seems still to be binding on the disciples.[5]

Marcion's Jesus, by contrast, comes into the world specifically to abolish the law and the prophets.[6] Marcion's interpretation, though

---

[1] 'There is a fourth-century tradition that Marcion was the scribe of John; and in the fifth-century *Acts of John*, Prochorus, disciple of John, claims to have been the scribe to whom John dictated the Gospel at Patmos.' Raymond E. Brown, op. cit., p.xcix, takes these and other legendary attributions as constituting 'an ancient recognition that the disciples of John contributed to the Gospel as scribes or even as editors'.

[2] Tertullian, the first church father of importance to write in Latin, defined Marcion's distinction between the two gods as follows: *alterum judicem, ferum, bellipotentem, alterum mitem, placidum et tantummodo bonum atque optimum* – 'the one a judge, fierce, mighty in war, the other mild, pacific, not only good but even perfect'. Cf. E. C. Blackman: *Marcion and His Influence*, London, 1948.

[3] Marcion's New Testament was to inspire, by ricochet, the New Testament we know. At the same time the church fathers took pains, once they had the political power, to destroy every copy of the earlier, heretical scripture. But enough survives from the polemic of his enemies for us to recognise that his lasting legacy was his rehabilitation of Paul, distrusted for more than a generation by the main current of orthodox preachers and writers.

[4] Matthew 5, 17–18. I have kept iota (the smallest letter in the Greek alphabet) and accent (for *keraia*), rather than try to translate them back into some Aramaic original: DS.

[5] Matthew 23, 2–3.

[6] *ouk elthon plerosai ton nomon, alla katalusai* – 'I did not come to fulfill the law, but to

condemned by the orthodox church, remains more logical than that of his enemies, who founded two contrasting scriptures in one cover as the Holy Bible. For in negating the dietary laws and abolishing compulsory circumcision for males, even the edited gospel of the church removed far more than minutiae from the Mosaic code.

It remains a puzzle why Marcion excluded John from his canon, particularly if he had worked as the author's scribe. Perhaps by the time he wrote the editorial process had introduced ideas into John which Marcion could not accept, and these changes may have been too widespread for him to excise, as he excised offending passages from Luke and Paul.[1] Among possible reasons we cannot include ignorance of the existence of the text. Early second-century fragments of John on papyrus[2] are older than fragments found from the other gospels.

The ambiguity as to Jesus's mission centres on two questions: did he think himself the messiah? and what was the content of his secret teaching?

The translators of the Septuagint had translated the Hebrew messiah as Christos, or Anointed. It was a title, not a proper name. By the time the four gospels achieved canonical status, Christos had become the routine surname for Jesus. So completely was he identified with the expected Jewish deliverer that the Arabic term for him in the Koran is *al-Masih*, 'the Messiah'.

Yet none of this proves that Jesus shared this view of himself and his role. Mark records that near Caesarea Philippi he asked his disciples who men thought him to be. They replied that some took him for the recently murdered Baptist, others for Elijah (who was expected to reappear in advance of the messiah) while yet others saw him as a prophet.

'But you, who do you say that I am?'
Peter replied, 'You are the Christ.'

And he enjoined them to tell no one about him. The other two synoptics repeat his strict orders that his disciples should keep quiet about the story that he was the messiah.[3]

---

abolish it' (cf. Blackman, op. cit.). The Gospel of the Ebionites has him coming into the world to abolish sacrificing (Epiphanius, *Panarion haer*. 30, 16, 5).

[1] Marcion repudiated the anti-feminism inherent in Judaism and ordained women to holy orders. Ascetic but consistently anti-nomian, he excised the passages in Paul which transmitted the older view, as well as passages in Paul condemning sexual relations between men.

[2] The papyrus fragments – of John 18, 31–33, 37–38 – are in the John Rylands Library, Manchester. Gr. P. 457.

[3] The one passage in the synoptic gospels where Jesus appears to confirm his messiahship carries little weight. 'Are you the Christ,' the High Priest asks him, 'the Son of the Blessed One?' 'I am,' he replies. Mark 14, 61–2. But the same chapter tells us that

Suetonius, the Roman historian, confirms that there were followers of Jesus in Rome as early as the reign of Claudius.[1] But he does not know Jesus as Christus. This evidence is important since, as *magister epistolarum*, or secretary, to Hadrian,[2] he had access to the imperial archives. When listing the reforms of Claudius (which included the extirpation of British Druidism) he adds,

> he drove from Rome the Jews causing constant trouble at the instigation of Chrestus.[3]

This expulsion – it can be dated to AD 49 – occurred less than twenty years after the Crucifixion. Suetonius does not explain precisely who 'the Jews' were. In all probability they were Greek-speaking gentiles converted to Judaism, such as were later to be satirised by Juvenal. But the archives on which he drew preserve a title for Jesus which was later to be discarded: a title without messianic connotations.

Chrestus (or in its Greek original, *chrêstos*) means gentle, kindly, good; it is, curiously, the equivalent of the common pharaonic title of Osiris, *Un-nefer*.[4] But this earlier title obviously became an embarrassment once the church had decided that Jesus had, in fact, been the messiah. The word itself became objectionable and seems to have been deliberately excised from certain passages in the gospels where it had occurred as an adjective and to have been replaced by words having a similar meaning. Evidence for this is found in two works by Justin Martyr, the first outstanding Christian apologist, written in the middle of the second century, the *Apology* and *Dialogue with Trypho*. In quotations from Matthew and Luke Justin used *chrêstos* where our modern Greek testaments have substituted alternatives.[5] The oldest New

---

Peter, the presumed source, was at this time 'down below in the courtyard'. He will not have heard what Jesus said and Jesus will not have had the opportunity to tell him. Hearsay and theology seem to have joined hands.

[1] AD 41–54.

[2] AD 117–138.

[3] *Judaeos, impulsore Chresto assidue tumultuantes, Roma expulit.*

[4] An inscription on Delos refers to *Chreste Isis*: cf. R. E. Witt: *Isis in the Graeco-Roman World*, Cornell University Press, 1971. Witt cites the phrase in note 65 to ch. XII, giving as source P. Roussel's *Les cultes égyptiens à Delos* (Paris, 1915–16).

[5] In *Apology* 15, 13 Justin has an important variant on what became the standard text: *Ginesthe de chrêstoi kai 'oiktirmones, 'os kai 'o pater 'umôn chrêstos 'esti.* In his Dialogue 96, 3a this reappears with minor variants: *Ginesthe chrêstoi kai 'oiktirmones, 'os kai 'o patêr 'umôn 'o 'ouranios.* Luke (6,36) changes this to: *Ginesthe 'oiktirmones kathôs 'o pater 'umôn oiktirmon 'estin.* Matthew similarly suppresses the adjective *chrêstos* or its plural form *chrêstoi*. The difference in meaning is slight. Luke in his modern form: 'Be compassionate as your Father is compassionate.' In Justin's form: 'Be gentle and compassionate as your heavenly Father is gentle.' Cf. A. F. Bellinzoni: *The Sayings of Jesus in the Writings of Justin Martyr*, Leiden, 1967. Bellinzoni establishes that Justin depended on synoptic or post-synoptic material and that his variants were not due to

Testament codex, the Sinaiticus, dating from the early fourth century, gives a reading which changes the familiar verse in Acts to:

It was at Antioch that the disciples were first called 'Chrestians'.[1]

Remarkable proof that 'gentle' was not only the original surname of Jesus – perhaps the Greek 'flower name' of his Alexandrian youth – but also a persistent title is provided by our oldest inscription from a building specifically put up by followers of Jesus. At Deir Ali, a village near Damascus, a 'synagogue of the Marcionites' survived into Byzantine times. Its dedicatory inscription is in Greek and can be dated to October, AD 318. It refers to

The Lord and Saviour Jesus Chrestos.

The name that Suetonius discovered in the archives was thus current two hundred and sixty-nine years after the riots in Claudian Rome.

If Jesus did not see his role as messianic, the argument, advanced by some modern theologians, that his ethics were designed simply for a brief period of transition before the establishment of the Kingdom, falls to the ground. His public ethical teaching was in any case paralleled in the teachings of the Pharisees, his one innovation being the injunction to love one's enemies.

But in his private teachings Jesus broached problems which had concerned but a handful of rabbis and had landed them in trouble. Akavia ben Mahalalel[2] had been excommunicated for maintaining positions on the law of purity regarded as heretical. 'Consider three things,' he had said, 'and you will not fall into the hands of transgression. Know where you come from and where you are going and before whom you are due to give account and reckoning. "Where you come from" – a putrid drop; "and where you are going" – to the place of dust, worm and maggot; "and before whom you are due to give account and reckoning": before the King of kings of kings, the Holy One, blessed is he.'[3] This has affinities with the formula of the Valentinian school of gnostics: 'What makes us free is the knowledge who we were, what we have become; where we come from, into what we have been thrown; where we speed to, from what we are redeemed.'[4] Yet the private instruction of Jesus took him still closer to the gnostics' teaching that

---

slips of memory. His variants were in the original synoptic texts but were edited out later. The word *chrêstos*, even as an adjective, had become embarrassing.

[1] Acts 11, 26. According to Albert C. Clark's *The Acts of the Apostles* (Oxford, 1933), Codex Sinaiticus is the oldest complete text; the even older but incomplete Michigan Papyrus does not, unfortunately, contain this particular passage.

[2] First century BC.

[3] Avot 3, 1.

[4] Jonas, p. 334: quoting Clement of Alexandria.

man comes from light and returns to light. The soul of man, in a recurrent image, is gold set in mud, the world of time and matter. Jesus's teachings that his kingdom is not of this world and that it is his followers' destiny to become, like himself, sons of God, echo this philosophy.[1]

The sea of ambiguity will not part for us like the Sea of Reeds. We must cross it with stepping stones and the most reliable are not the things he said (which can be edited or censored) but the actions that he took after selecting the first small nucleus of male disciples.

---

[1] 'I tell you most emphatically, the man who believes in me will do the same works I do and will do even greater, since I am going to the Father.' John 14, 12: DS.

CHAPTER ELEVEN

Wine And Blood

Three days after Jesus had chosen his first five disciples, there was a wedding at Cana in Galilee, Nathanael's home village. 'The mother of Jesus was there,' John tells us, 'and Jesus and his disciples were invited too. The wine running out, his mother said to him, "They have no wine." Jesus retorted, "What is it to me and you, woman? My hour has not come yet." His mother said to the servants, "Now do whatever he tells you." There were six stone jars waiting nearby, for the ablutions customary among Jews, of a capacity between twenty and thirty gallons: Jesus told the servants, "Fill the jars with water." And they filled them up. "Now draw some out and take it to the man in charge of the feast." When this man tasted the water, which had turned to wine, and knowing nothing of its origins (for only the servants who had drawn it knew) he called the bridegroom and said, "People usually offer the good wine first, and when everyone's tight, produce the inferior. But you have kept back the good wine till now."'[1]

The story occurs only in John and this is easily explained. While the fourth gospel incorporates a personal reminiscence, Mark's eye-witness source is Simon Peter. The wedding took place four days after Jesus had met Peter, whose mother-in-law Jesus was shortly to cure of a fever.[2] If this lady was sick at the time Peter first joined Jesus, it would account for Peter's absence from Cana. Even without such a domestic upset, a man with a trade would have found it less easy to drop everything for a walking tour in Galilee than someone like his younger brother, Andrew (who had already attached himself to the Baptist), or the unnamed disciple. The dramatic experience at Cana would thus have been precisely the kind of thing which an old man would have remembered seventy years later; at the time it may well have clinched his faith. Mark on the other hand would have received

[1] John 2, 1–11: DS.
[2] Mark 1, 29–31.

no such vivid report from a Peter who had not been present.[1]

The disciples who accompanied Jesus to the wedding will have included Nathanael, Andrew, Philip and the unnamed disciple. Even this small group will have constituted a considerable addition to the feast, which would last three days or longer. The guests would be entertained and lodged but expected to bring presents of a value precisely determined by Galilean tradition. Mary may have feared that her son was unaware of this rural tradition.

Other details confirm the impression that Jesus was not deeply rooted in the province. His address was unknown to the Baptist's group; living by the lake, he seems detached from any family house at Nazareth. A lack of intimacy is apparent between him and Mary on the one hand, and his half brothers on the other, since they are not described as attending the wedding. This lack of family ties, a leitmotif in John, will resound for the last time at Golgotha, where, in violence to the Levant's familial ties, Jesus will not commit Mary to the care of his kith or kin.

But Mary herself had grown up to know of Galilean etiquette in relation to gifts: an outlay which the groom would return when his guest duly married in his turn.[2] Her son and his party would have been despised, she herself dishonoured, if they proved empty-handed. From previous experience Mary must have known that Jesus had paranormal powers.

Jesus's ability and willingness to produce good wine imposes contrasted questions: was it an interruption of natural law? What was its significance?

John sees in it 'the first of the signs given by Jesus':[3] miraculous proof of who he is. Fifteen credulous centuries were to class it with the miracle of St Joseph of Copertino flying round his church. The first historical novels about Jesus, written in the rationalistic eighteenth century, proposed naturalistic explanations of what seemed miraculous. Thus, the wine could have been secretly brought in advance and concealed till the right moment. But the ability of someone with the powerful personality attested in all accounts of Jesus (aware too, of the

[1] A further possibility is that Peter was not among the first disciples to be recruited. His early inclusion in John could be the work of an editor anxious to stress the priority of the man whom the church was to regard as *primus inter pares*, the first of a line of infallible successors. Mark's time structure gives this possibility some support. Mark sets the call of Peter *after* the Baptist's arrest and Jesus's appearance in Galilee, while John has Jesus visiting Jerusalem with disciples, who baptise in his name, *before* the Baptist was imprisoned. (Contrast Mark 1, 14–16 with John 3, 22–24.)
[2] For a learned discussion of the customs relating to weddings in Galilee, and the question of what category of guest was required to bring a present, see *Law in the New Testament*: J. Duncan M. Derrett, London, 1970: chapter 10.
[3] John 2, 11.

magical techniques current in the Levant), to convince inebriated villagers that the jars dragged in after midnight held wine not water, finds
many parallels in the annals of suggestion. From the Indian rope trick
to the experiments of modern hypnotists there is ample confirmation
of the hallucination which can be accepted by the suggestible. This
particular wonder takes us, however, to the heart of his mission.

The cultivation of the wheat-plant and vine had symbolised the
legendary activity of Osiris. Before the ascendancy of this god,
Egyptians had been hunters and meat-eaters; Osiris taught them agri-
culture and with it civilisation. Bread and wine were alternatives to the
sacrificial elements used in carnivorous temples. They marked as decisive a break with the rituals of Mithras. As a sign, the production of
wine from water was as impressive as the wondrous feat suggested by
the tempter, though far more agreeable in its content. Since a man can
only be tempted by something to his taste, Jesus evidently had a yearn-
ing for applause and power which he resisted by an act of will. John
says that the wonder caused his disciples to believe in him (further evidence that the primary enthusiasm of Philip and Nathanael was
written in later), then adds: 'After this he went down to Capernaum
with his mother and the brothers, but they stayed there only a few
days.'[1] 'The brothers' refers to his disciples, not to the sons of Joseph.
They share with him the sun-father who revealed himself over the
Jordan as they have shared the bread and wine which are to become his
particular symbols. Jesus then leaves Galilee to attend the Passover in
Jerusalem.

From the way John tells the story, this would seem the first time
Jesus had set foot in David's city. If Jesus had grown up in Palestine he
would, like other Jews, have made the effort to celebrate major feasts
in the holy city.

Herod's temple was a material wonder, though never finally completed, of the Hellenised Jewish world. Close to, its atmosphere was
impressive and alien. Its monolithic columns supported capitals as
jungly as the wreaths which Romanised trenchermen wore at dinner.
The Herodian style incorporated elements to be found in the law
courts, theatres and temples of the chief Palestinian cities, whether
Scythopolis at the head of the Vale of Esdraelon, Caesarea by the Mediterranean, Tiberias by the lake or those of the Ten Cities east of the
Jordan. Jesus would have found similar architecture if he had led his
disciples to the Rhine, the Rhone or the dunes confronting the chalk
cliffs of Britain.

The temple's ponderous foundations shared the strength of the

---

[1] For the Cana episode, see John 2, 1–12. I follow the Jerusalem Bible in its reading of
verse 12 and in its contention that 'the "brothers" are not blood brothers of Jesus but
the inner circle of his first disciples'.

roads and vaulted bridges that linked middle eastern towns to the imperial network. The temple's inner shrine, the holy of holies, had been built by the hands of priests, in the ancient manner. It mustered the same numinous darkness as an Egyptian shrine. But while rows of standing statues watched the tenebrous interiors of Thebes or Memphis, the shrine of Yahweh, the god who claimed to be everywhere, was empty. Yet the invisible deity retained the passions of wrath and hunger and the temple's function was to placate and feed him. When Solomon sacrificed, he did so on an outcrop of rock once used for threshing. This had become the fundament of an altar of holocaust, piled up like a truncated pyramid from stones unshaped by metal. Herod's temple centred on sacrifice no less than Solomon's. When the wind was blowing, the fumes of combustion swirled far beyond the city limits. Like the fumes dissolving sweat in a Roman steam bath, the sacred smoke expunged the people's sins. Temple expiation, it need hardly be added, cost money.

Those who benefited included priests, the suppliers of livestock and poultry, and those who took their percentage on changing secular money for sacred. The coins in use outside bore the head of the emperor, a gentile claiming to be the heir of a god and destined for deification at his own funeral. Such money, and all gentiles, were taboo in the sacred enclosure. A low barrier of marble with warnings written in Greek and other tongues threatened death to those who intruded beyond it.

Fresh from Cana, where his powers had entranced the revellers, he alarmed his new disciples by denouncing the sale of animals and the pious money-changing. If the 'something' within were good, that something could not delight in the froth of blood or the burning of lamb-flesh. What pleased the god, one of his prophets had said, was a humble and contrite spirit.

Making a small flail from cord Jesus chased out the sellers and overturned the money-changers' benches.

What astonishes us, as it must have astonished his companions, is the passivity of those he assailed. Someone who had not only studied Nilotic magic, but studied its practitioners, *could* have facilitated such a demonstration by bribing the men affected in advance. The explanation more probably lies in the personal authority that Jesus exerted, which was much more than the confidence a travelled man can display to the stay-at-home. But his action had Egyptian echoes. The flail was one of the two symbols of Osiris.[1] His disgust with animal sacrifice recalls us the fellahin who burnt down the Hebrew temple at Elephantine.

---

[1] The other symbol was the shepherd's crook. Jesus in his role of Good Shepherd was to be associated with this symbol, too.

John records at the temple an exchange of words of great value to the historian. When the Jews demand a sign to justify his action, Jesus retorts that he could rebuild the temple in three days if they destroyed it. John then makes one of those factual insertions which punctuate his poetry.

For forty-six years this sanctuary has been abuilding. And you in three days will raise it up?[1]

Herod had started reconstructing the temple in BC 19. We can therefore date this incident with some confidence to the spring of AD 28.

[1] John 2, 20: DS.

CHAPTER TWELVE

The Puzzle Of Narrative Structure

Peter's absence, whatever its cause, would explain why Mark, and following him Matthew and Luke, put the action in the temple just before the end of Jesus's mission, and not at the beginning. It was too dramatic to overlook.

But, some may protest: Peter would surely have informed Mark fully on what happened in the final week? This is to ignore human psychology. Peter's last days with Jesus were not of the kind to infuse the pride which can sometimes balance grief. In tragic events his role was inglorious. The man nicknamed 'Rock' had wobbled into a panicky denial hardly distinguishable from repudiation. He had then made off, leaving the unnamed disciple as the one male follower to accompany Jesus to the cross. For Peter, looking back on this record was as difficult as staring at the sun. For the sequence of events which led to the interrogations and death of Jesus, John thus provides the most coherent narrative.

According to John, after the demonstration in the temple, Jesus took his first disciples back to Galilee through the Samarian hills. Peter might not have countenanced this route: strict Jews so much objected to travelling through Samaria that they usually travelled north by the road up the east bank of the Jordan, so avoiding contact with a despised minority. Peter's absence would thus explain why the Samarian journey is not mentioned in the synoptic gospels. The first small group of disciples had reached a stage in their development where they had begun to question the assumptions of Palestinian Jewry. In the event the Samarian journey took them well beyond the ethical instruction found so plentifully in the synoptics. Jesus defies convention and, to a Samaritan woman whose morality was that of a whore, imparts some of the most beautiful words in the New Testament. The woman has come to draw water from the local well. Jesus, whose disciples have gone in to the nearby town to buy food, asks her for a drink.

The Samaritan woman said to him, 'How do you, a Jew, ask me, a Samaritan female, for a drink?' Jews do not, in fact, consort with

Samaritans. Jesus answered: 'If you only knew what God is offering and who is asking you to let him drink, you would have asked him and he would have given you living water.'

'You have no bucket, sir,' she replied, 'and the well is deep. How could you get this living water? Are you a greater man than our ancestor Jacob who gave us this well and drank from it himself, with his sons and his cattle?' Jesus replied: 'Everyone who drinks this water will get thirsty again; but whoever drinks from the water that I shall give him will not thirst throughout eternity. It will turn into an inner spring, founting into eternal life.'[1]

It is as hard to adjust such symbolic actions to the deluded messiah of an ethnocentric cult as it is to fit the sage of arcane teaching into the ecclesiastical drama of cruelty in which a god demands the blood of his son to expunge the world's sins.

We begin to understand how the confusion could have arisen when we scrutinise the methods by which the synoptics seem to have composed their gospels. Despite Matthew's apostolic name, none of the three had seen Jesus. They show little knowledge of the country in which he conducted his mission. Their materials were secondary, chapbooks in which earlier admirers had recorded more sayings than incidents. Germanic investigation of the New Testament in the nineteenth century proved that, apart from Mark, who has his own list of sayings, Matthew and Luke shared a source.[2] In addition Matthew and Luke each had material peculiar to himself alone. Then as late as 1945 an Egyptian peasant stumbled on a large jar containing texts which had been buried in the fourth century from fear of a persecuting church. The discovery, important for what it confirmed about gnosticism, also gave a vivid idea of the form which the building blocks of scripture must have had. One document in particular, *The Gospel of Thomas*, preserved the Coptic version of a work known already in fragmentary Greek. While the content shows a freshness lacking in more edited texts, the form is characteristic. Thomas begins:

These are the secret words which Didymus Judas Thomas wrote. And he said: He who finds the explanation of these words will not taste death. Jesus said: He who seeks must not stop seeking until he finds, and when he finds he will be bewildered; and if he is not bewildered, he will marvel, and will be king over the All.
Jesus said: If those who lead you say to you, Lo, the kingdom is in heaven, then the birds of heaven will precede you; if they say to you, It is in the sea, then the fish will precede you. But the kingdom is within you and outside you. When you know yourselves, then you

[1] John 4, 7–14: DS.
[2] Biblical scholars know this by the letter Q, from the German word *Quelle*, a source.

will be known; and you will know that you are the sons of the living Father. But if you do not know yourselves, then you are in poverty, and you are the poverty.[1]

The teaching has evident affinities with the mainstream of Hellenic philosophy as it flows back to Socrates and Plato. The Coptic in which it was written was a dialect of the Egyptian populace; it was written in borrowed Greek letters with the addition of seven other letters derived from pharaonic. Because they lacked a literary tradition, the Copts borrowed many words from Greek. There are seven such borrowings in the brief passage quoted. Two are of interest. *Thalassa*, for sea, reminds us that to Egyptians, as to the author of the Hymn of the Pearl, the Nile was the sea, and for the larger ocean they needed to borrow. More significant, the word used for explanation is *hermeneia*, a term used since Plato for interpretation 'of what has been spoken more or less obscurely by others'.[2]

Coptic *Thomas* contains a hundred and fourteen Sayings, or *Logoi*. They have no narrative framework. Sayings are simply introduced by the formula, 'Jesus said', or 'He said'. The Jesus of Thomas is living: but not in ordinary time or ordinary matter. He is not exalted as an ethical teacher or legislator. His sayings have the puzzling nature of Zen riddles. The puzzler is not an actor in secular history. He purveys no doctrine of atonement, let alone national liberation. There is no suggestion of him planning to go to Jerusalem to die. He is an enlightener who imparts flashes of revolutionary gnosis.

Mark and the other two synoptics must have handled similar collections of sayings when they composed their gospels. Jerusalem had fallen and the first disciples had begun to die off. Perhaps inevitably they decided to weave the public and private sayings into a narrative.

Where did they get its structure, and how true is it to history?

Writing between AD 145 and 160, Justin Martyr claims to have consulted certain Memoirs of the Apostles. But the first critical attempt to describe the composition of the gospels comes to us from Eusebius, whose ten-volume *History of the Christian Church* was published in 324–325. Eusebius was tendentious on many points. His view that Matthew was written by the disciple of that name, that it was the first gospel, and was originally in Hebrew finds little support today. But Eusebius recognised that the synoptics basically cover only the single year after the Baptist's arrest. He also felt it necessary to explain John's

[1] The translation by B. M. Metzger appears between pp. 517 & 530 of *Synopsis Quattuor Evangeliorum*, ed. Kurt Aland, Stuttgart; 9th revision, 1976. The original puts the seven words of Greek incorporated in the Coptic text in brackets.

[2] See Grimm's Wilke's *Clavis Novi Testamenti; A Greek-English Lexicon of the New Testament*; revised J. H. Thayer, Edinburgh, 1961.

motives for writing. 'The three previous gospels were distributed to all, including himself; he apparently welcomed them and testified to their truth but pointed out that their narratives omitted an account of the first part of Christ's mission and preaching.' What he tells us about Mark is a mixture of the credible and the untrue. 'Mark was the first to be sent to preach in Egypt the gospel which he had also put into writing. He was also the first to establish churches in Alexandria itself. The first wave of converts was so great and their asceticism conducted on so philosophic a plane that Philo thought it right to describe their conduct, assemblies, meals and other details of their way of life. Tradition relates that he visited Rome in the reign of Claudius to speak to Peter, at that time preaching in the City.'[1] Eusebius is mistaken in identifying the Therapeutae, about whom Philo did write, with the early Christians. But the information about Mark which he derived from Papias is important. 'Mark became Peter's interpreter and wrote accurately all that he remembered, not, indeed, in the right sequence, of what the Lord said or did. For he had neither heard the Lord nor followed him, but later on, as I said, followed Peter. The latter instructed him as necessity demanded but without making, as it were, an arrangement of the Lord's oracles; so that Mark himself cannot be blamed for thus writing down single points as he remembered them.'

The problem thus remains of knowing where Peter's viewpoint influenced Mark and where the latter's text has been influenced, or edited, in the direction of what was rapidly becoming orthodox opinion. For once the Jewish authorities in Jerusalem had been defeated by the Romans, the church began to claim that it subsumed the tradition of the synagogue. The result was what may be called, not too fancifully, a brand of anti-Semitic Semitism.

The narrative of the gospel-writers made no attempt to present a coherent month-by-month, let alone day-by-day, record of the period culminating in the passion: a year, in the case of the synoptics, a period encompassing three Passovers in the case of John. Narrative simply provides a thread on which to string 'single points', as Papias had termed the short, detachable passages of scripture which theologians today called 'pericopes'. If our only source were the gospels, we should oscillate between the view that Jesus saw himself as a messiah who liberates through his death and the view that he saw himself as a revealer of specific gnosis. Fortunately there is other evidence to indicate which view was held by Jesus.

For the gospels are not the earliest New Testament writings. Apart from Paul's letters, which show no interest in the physical appearance of Jesus and not much more in the sequence of his everyday actions, the Acts of the Apostles, a compendium of uneven materials plausibly

[1] Eusebius: *Ecclesiastical History*, II, xvi; Loeb, Vol. 1: p. 145.

ascribed to Luke and dating from roughly the same period as the composition of the gospels, preserves a passage which seems older than Paul's first letter.

In the winter of AD 36/7[1] a young, Greek-speaking Jew named Stephen was lynched for his public fidelity to Jesus. Stephen is included in Acts for three things: his work in the young community, his speech as an apologist, and his death as a witness, or martyr. The followers of Jesus had already broken into various sub-groups. Hellenised Jews who had settled in the holy city after living in the diaspora formed one such sub-group and included Stephen. The ideas of Jesus were easily assimilable to those who spoke Greek and Stephen was only the latest of a line of supporters with Greek names. It began with Philip, Andrew and Nicodemus and was to be continued by Timothy, Jason, Sosipater, Erastos and many more. The Hellenistic converts complained that their dependents fared less well in the collectivised distribution of food than those of Palestinian Jews. To heal the rift, seven Hellenists were chosen to supervise the distributions. Stephen was one. But he was also an eloquent spokesman for his vision of Jesus and his role. This irked those Hellenised Jews who adhered to the Law and, according to Acts, they induced informers to denounce him for blaspheming Moses and God. Much like Jesus before him, Stephen was dragged to the temple. The Sanhedrin were there informed that 'this man is always making speeches against this Holy Place and the Law. We have heard him say that Jesus the Nazarene is going to destroy this Place and alter the traditions that Moses handed down to us.'[2]

Like the rest of the New Testament, Acts is designed to persuade. But even so, it preserves a decipherable indication of the charges against Stephen, and of his answer, even if the account is biased and the defence Stephen mounts is idealised. The false witnesses were probably merely hostile. Stephen's speech has to be read in the Greco-Roman context; even secular historians such as Thucydides and Tacitus did not claim to give literal transcriptions of the orations of great men. In Stephen's case, the scene was one of menacing tumult. The pen of a note-taking observer would have trembled. Furthermore, Acts presents Stephen's speech as an exemplary sermon, an early Christian *midrash*. Its thirteen hundred words are interlarded with scriptural references, an average of two to every three lines. But behind this reworking of a desperate, last-act speech, important arguments resound. They have the same sense of authenticity as other awkward passages. Stephen, after stressing that God is localised in no

---

[1] This date is conjecture by the editors of the *Jerusalem Bible*, among others.
[2] The episode dealing with Stephen occupies the last paragraph of Acts 6 and all of Acts 7.

particular place, concentrates on the career of the very law-giver he was accused of blaspheming. But his charges, that in their attitude to Moses the Jews had resisted the Holy Spirit as they resisted it now, culminated in words intolerable to his hearers:

> Can you name one prophet your forefathers did not persecute? In the past they killed those who foretold the coming of the Just One, and now you have betrayed him and killed him.[1]

Enraged, his accusers clapped their hands over their ears and dragged him out of the city walls for stoning.[2] Those who have witnessed this horrific method of execution debate whether its worst feature is the extrusion of the eyes or the dislocation of the jawbone. But the author of Acts, opening two centuries in which the persecutor was to become the church's recruiting sergeant, sentimentalises Stephen's end:

> Then he knelt down and cried out, Lord, do not charge this sin against them. And with these words he fell asleep.[3]

Apart from the evidence that Jesus implanted passionate loyalty in some of those who heard him, this speech is of biographical significance in four respects. Stephen compares Jesus with Moses, not with the messianic David. He refers to Moses becoming a man of power in word and action thanks to his Egyptian[4] studies. Stephen names Jesus as 'the Just One', a term nearer to Chreŝtos than Christos. The violence which prevents him completing his account of the death of Moses suggests that Freud's secret of the Old Testament, that Moses had been murdered by the followers of Yahweh, was known to Stephen and his accusers.

---

[1] Acts 7, 52:DS.

[2] The manner in which an offender should be stoned had been meticulously defined. (178 Sanhedrin 6, 1–4). 'When he was four cubits from the place of stoning they stripped off his clothes. A man is kept covered in front and a woman both in front and behind. The place of stoning was twice the height of a man. One of the witnesses knocked him down on his loins; if he turned over on his heart the witness turned him over again on his loins. If he straightway died, that sufficed; but if not, the second took the stone and dropped it on his heart. If he straightway died, that sufficed; but if not, he was stoned by all Israel, for it is written *The hand of the witnesses shall be first upon him to put him to death and afterward the hand of all the people*' (Deut. 17,7). Some authorities, such as Rabbi Eliezer, demanded that the dead man should then be hanged, so as to incur the curse attached to hanging. In that case, the corpse was hanged briefly by its hands. Rabbi Jose is quoted for the information that 'the beam was made to lean against a wall and one hanged the corpse thereon as the butchers do'.

[3] Acts 7, 60: DS.

[4] Acts 7, 22.

CHAPTER THIRTEEN

Jesus And The Jews

Although Jesus did not finally see himself as the messiah, he had certainly pondered the role's applicability to the mission signalled by the Voice. His rejection of the role did not mean that he took no position on the collective concerns of the Jews. Yet these obsessive and divisive concerns have been ignored as much by those enlisting Jesus in the cause of evanescent modernities as by those portraying him in a never-never land modelled on Tuscany.

Parts of first-century Palestine supported a Jewish majority: chiefly mountainous Judaea and inland Galilee. The coastal plain was predominantly pagan while Scythopolis, the important city at the head of the valley of Esdraelon, had a mixed Hellenistic population. Palestinian Jews were as fragmented as the country. Some, in particular the temple authorities and the Sadducee sect, sought an accommodation with Rome. Others agitated in a perennial dissidence which was to lead to the disastrous revolt of AD 66. Those who resisted the empire of Caesar did not do so simply as a suppressed nationality, such as the tribes Augustus had subjugated at the junction for a special purpose of Italy and Gaul, but as a people convinced that God had set them apart from humanity. The riot which flared in other provinces, even such armed revolts as that of East Anglia's Iceni, were storms of an afternoon compared with what Jewish zealots saw as a cosmic struggle. Unlike other rebels, they expected intervention from on high.

The attitude of Jesus to the Jewish version, to the confidence which gave their revolt its incentive and ferocity, is as ambiguous as anything else in his career, depending very much on which evangelist is writing.

Matthew's gospel embodies obvious contradictions. His somewhat schizophrenic hero both upholds the law to its last iota, and overrules it when convenient. Matthew wrote at a time when circumcision, the dietary laws and Sabbath observance were no longer seen as binding on Christians. One remarkable chapter, the fifteenth, shows Jesus as simultaneously against the law and yet attached to ethnic exclusivity.

The chapter opens with scribes and Pharisees from Jerusalem rebuking Jesus for letting his disciples abstain from washing their hands before they eat. Jesus restates the law:

> What goes into the mouth does not make a man profane: it was what
> comes out of the mouth that profanes him.[1]

A sensible view, but not that of the Mosaic code, which meticulously
lists those things whose consumption, or even touch, pollutes a man.[2]

Later in the same chapter Jesus visits south Lebanon. A local
woman embarrasses his disciples by clamouring for him to heal her
daughter.

> 'Get rid of her, as she's screaming behind us.'
> He replied: 'I was not sent to anyone except the lost sheep of the
> House of Israel.'
> But the woman had come up and was prostrating herself to him.
> 'Lord,' she said, 'help me.'
> 'It is not right,' he answered, 'to take the children's food and throw
> it to pet dogs.'
> 'True, Sir,' she replied; 'but even pet dogs can eat the scraps that fall
> from their masters' table.'[3]

The Greek word here translated as 'pet dogs' is *kounaria*; the dog has
remained a source of middle eastern insult into modern times.

The question posed by the story is not the miracle in which Jesus
heals her daughter but the authenticity of his words. Even if *kounaria*
is an affectionate diminutive, it is hard to reconcile a Jesus who compares non-Jews to dogs with the Jesus of Luke, who significantly does
not use the story. The opposition is as sharp as between the puritanical
nationalism of the Essenes and the universalistic philosophy of the
Therapeutae.

The central chapters of John depict by contrast a Jesus who had little
time for the chauvinistic concerns implicit in Mark and Matthew. The
Prologue to the fourth gospel had already proclaimed a universal
Logos, 'the true light that enlightens all men'. At the Feast of Tabernacles in Jerusalem Jesus declares:

> Yet a little time I am with you and then I go back to him who sent

---

[1] The Greek word *koinos* (which also gives us *koinê*, the common language) is translated 'unclean' by the *Jerusalem Bible*; the Authorised Version speaks of defilement.
[2] Leviticus 11: Jews are forbidden to eat or even handle: the meat of the camel, the
hare, the pig; anything that lives in water but lacks fins or scales; among winged creatures, the tawny vulture, the griffon, the osprey, the kite, all kinds of buzzard and
raven, the ostrich, the screech owl, the seagull, all kinds of hawk, horned owl, night
owl, cormorant, barn owl, ibis, pelican, white vulture, stork, heron, hoopoe and bat;
also a variety of insects.
[3] Matthew 15, 24–27: DS.

me. You will seek me and you will not find me.[1]

The Jews (John does not distinguish between Pharisees, scribes and Sadducees) inquire:

Is he going to visit the Greek diaspora and will he teach the Greeks?

As we shall find on a yet more important occasion, words that puzzle Jewish hearers are clues to hidden elements in this extraordinary man. It is probable that to Palestinian Jews the 'diaspora of the Greeks' meant *par excellence* Alexandria. Jesus's proclamation of himself a few verses later as the 'light of the world'[2] may show how much he was in tune with their thoughts. The metaphor could convey an unconscious memory of the city celebrated for its lighthouse.

These exchanges about his origin, destination and nature turn to an acerbic discussion of paternity. Jesus derides the Jewish claim to derive from Abraham while they have a dig at him in their retort, 'We were not born of prostitution.'[3] Jesus continues:

You are from the devil, your father and his lusts you are eager to fulfill. He was a man-slayer from the beginning.[4]

Unless he is simply bandying abuse, Jesus is asserting that far from worshipping the true god, the Jews, or their law, derive from the spirit which on three occasions he identifies as 'the lord of this world',[5] the spirit which tempted him in the desert.

When the Jews respond – 'Are we not right in saying that you are a Samaritan and possessed by a demon?'[6] – they, too, are either bandying abuse or are associating him with an incipient gnostic movement in Samaria, whose most famous figure was Simon Magus. If Samaritan is used in this sense, their question implies that Jesus was a stranger to them. His Galilean origin was certainly not self-evident, as it was in the case of Simon Peter.

The dispute ends with Jesus declaring:

Your father Abraham rejoiced that he would see my Day. He saw it and was glad.

To which the Jews reply:

You are not fifty yet, and you have seen Abraham?

[1] John 7, 33–34: DS.
[2] John 9, 5.
[3] John 8, 41–42: DS.
[4] John 8, 44: DS.
[5] John 12, 31; 14, 30; 16, 11. The phrase is *ho archon tou kosmou toutou*.
[6] John 8, 48: DS.

I assert most truly: Before Abraham was, I am.[1]

Jesus thus denies Jewish uniqueness; so far from being a spiritual elite, the children of the law are convicted of diabolic paternity. To which the Jews reply that Jesus is raving mad. Why bother to listen?

This pattern of mounting conflict is duplicated in the lives of other heretics and prophets. An outsider does not reach his hemlock or torture-chamber in one dramatic week. Months or years, in the case of Socrates, convince the Athenians that the philosopher does not believe in the state religion and corrupts the youth; al-Hallaj, the ninth-century mystic from Baghdad is an old man by the time he is painfully killed for equating himself with God.

'He could not stay in Judaea, because the Jews were out to kill him.'[2] People pointed him out in Jerusalem: 'Isn't this the man they want to kill?'[3] After returning to Galilee, he revisits Jerusalem for the Feast of Tabernacles. 'They would have arrested him then. . . .' A few days later, on the last and most important day of the Feast: 'Some would have liked to apprehend him, but no one in fact laid hands on him.'[4] The Pharisees send the temple police but, overawed by his personality, they return empty-handed.[5] After his argumentation with Jewish disputants, the latter picked up stones to throw at him, but Jesus inconspicuously left the Temple.[6] He is again in Jerusalem for the winter feast of the Dedication of the Temple. Again outraged Jews pick up stones in order to lynch him. Jesus mentions the good deeds he has done. Which of them incurs the penalty of stoning? But the Jews reply that they are not stoning him for good works but for the crime of blasphemy.

You are only a man yet make yourself out to be a god.[7]

The conflict between Jesus and orthodox Jews was, as so often in such cases, between two sincerely held but mutually exclusive visions of the world. In this case the results of the collision were to be momentous.

[1] John 8, 56–57: DS.
[2] John 7, 1: DS.
[3] John 7, 25: DS.
[4] John 7, 44: DS.
[5] John 7, 32.
[6] John 8, 59.
[7] John 10, 31–34: DS.

CHAPTER FOURTEEN

The Jews And Jesus

Although Jesus was to find his most lethal opponents in Jerusalem, he was also to anger orthodox Jews in Galilee. The anger was not due to suspicion that Jesus might be claiming to be the messiah. For such claims were neither rare nor considered blasphemous; Davidic pretenders made no claims to deity and since most of them ended unhappily, the prevailing attitude was one of pity.

To the scribes and Pharisees who came down from Jerusalem to investigate him, Jesus was suspect on two main grounds. The first was that he seemed to misrepresent the law which God revealed through Moses. Yet thanks to the nature of the religion which the Temple served and the Pharisees defended, machinery for persecuting the heterodox was rudimentary. 'The peculiarity of the Jewish law is that it is pre-eminently *a law of ritual*. It seeks in the first place to establish by law in what manner God desires to be honoured, what sacrifices are to be offered to Him, what festivals are to be kept in His honour, how His priests are to be maintained, and what religious rites in general are to be observed. All other matters occupy but a small space in comparison with this.'[1] Whereas priests in some other religions have been assessed for the correctness of their opinions on a range of doctrine, 'the primary requisite in a Jewish priest was evidence of his pedigree'.[2] And however pure his family tree, he was disqualified if he had any bodily defect.[3] The enemies of Jesus thus occupied an intellectual world very different from that which produced the Holy Inquisition. According to another authority, Jewish energies, during the five centuries preceding the birth of Jesus, were 'wholly focussed on one object, that of retaining their religious individuality at all costs. This all-absorbing interest led to the production of two significant phenomena, brought about, however, more by the force of circumstances than

[1] Emil Schürer: *A History of the Jewish People in the Time of Christ*, Edinburgh, 1885: Div. II, Vol. 1, p. 337. Nahum N. Glatzer, who edits a recent re-issue of Schürer, criticises his author for a 'failure to see the non-legal, decidedly internalized aspects of Jewish piety'. But this criticism does not invalidate the argument here, which relates to Judaism as an institution.

[2] Ibid, p.214.

[3] Ibid, p.210.

any preconceived plan'.[1] These were the organisation, partly political, of the priestly caste, and then the attentive devotion to the strict observance of the law, which had come to be regarded as the unbreakable barrier which separated Jew from gentile, and as the guardian of the faith and hope of Israel.

Jesus threatened the two poles of Jewish authority: the priests who served and profited from the Temple; and the teachers who defended the Mosaic code while often humanising it by reference to an oral tradition. But what angered the instructed elite attracted the populace. The Baptist had already provided a mode of self-purgation less costly than temple sacrifice. The Jerusalem clergy tended to despise the simple people from Galilee for their minimal practice, let alone understanding, of the complex law. This prejudice derived in part from history. Galilee's Jews had been evacuated, for the sake of safety, during the wars of the Maccabees against the Syrians; it is improbable that it had been reconstituted by those of unquestioned Jewish pedigree. And even in Galilee it was society's outcasts – former prostitutes like Mary of Magdala or tax-gatherers like Levi – who formed the bulk of his following.

If heresy, with his claim to forgive sins as a main ingredient, was the first accusation against Jesus, a second involved the factor which had first won him fame. His ability to work miracles, to chase out devils, underpinned his middle eastern reputation for several generations. Professor Morton Smith has calculated that over two hundred gospel events involve miraculous elements.[2] These outrun the hundred or so wonders in the pagan work most akin to the gospels, the third-century *Life of Apollonius of Tyana* by Philostratus. The miracles of Jesus are several times more numerous than those recorded of any Old Testament figure. Besides healings and exorcisms, they included the apparent ability to multiply food, to control the climate, to walk on water and to transmute water into wine.

In their nature the miracles of Jesus, however impressive, were not unique: but their number and attestation by many observers won him unparalleled fame. The idea that a powerful sage could achieve such things was well established. Moses and Elijah had worked prodigies of healing and destruction. In the fifth century BC the Sicilian philosopher Empedocles had claimed that he could teach his pupils to stay the winds and revive the dead. He did not dispute the popular belief that he was a god made flesh.[3]

The healing methods used by Jesus conformed to the medical

[1] Ch. Guignebert: *The Jewish World in the Time of Jesus*, New York, 1939: p.49.
[2] Morton Smith: op.cit., p. 109.
[3] E. R. Dodds: *The Greeks and the Irrational*, University of California Press, 1959: p. 45. Empedocles wrote: *ego d' 'umin' 'ambrotos, 'ouketi thnetos*.

theories of the first-century Levant. These presupposed that the invisible world thronged with demons at the beck of the evil one. They hovered in the air, haunting by preference waterless places and the neighbourhood of tombs. They were the prime causes of sin, disease and death. To be sick was, indeed, to be possessed by an evil spirit. Such spirits could pass from one person to another and from human beings into animals.[1] To heal was thus to exorcise and Jesus as exorcist had no known rival.

Nor were his physical methods peculiar to him, his place or his time. An incident in the life of the prophet Muhammad attests the persistence of such practices at least into the seventh century:

> On the day of the battle of Khaybar, the Prophet said, 'I am going to give the flag to a man to whom God will assure success, a man who loves God and his Messenger and who is loved by them.' All night people wondered which among them would be chosen. The Prophet called for Ali ibn Abi Talib: but was told that Ali's eyes were troubling him. He made him come, spat in his eyes and made invocation for him. Ali was healed and carried the flag.[2]

The miracles which fill the early chapters of the three synoptic gospels occurred in a society lacking hospitals and what we would recognise as physicians. The dusty climate helped many kinds of illness to flourish, particularly of the eyes; the absence of psychiatric institutions meant that town and country teemed with unstable personalities.

If in public Jesus healed the sick, in private, with his disciples, he experimented with symbols that expressed his deepest feelings about the relationship of the everyday world with the alternative cosmos ruled by the god of light. If a cold-eyed alien had assessed his actions and metaphors, he would have found them much closer to the older, more poetic religions of the middle east than to the ethnocentric monotheism of the Israel that had returned from the Babylonian captivity. Jesus was aware of a kingdom which interpenetrated the here and now but was distinct from it. The here and now was characterised by sickness, violence, greed. It was cankered at its heart and the laws which ruled it were part of that canker. In the gnostic term, this world was a sea of mud; in a striking phrase Jesus likened its devotees to the bleached grass of summer destined to fire ovens. A soul trapped by this world's lures forgot its destiny and place of origin.

[1] Cf. R. Campbell Thompson: *Semitic Magic, Its Origins and Development*, London, 1908.
[2] Toufic Fahd: *La Divination Arabe; Etudes Religieuses, Sociologiques et Folkloriques sur le Milieu Natif de l'Islam*, Leiden, 1966: p. 90.

You are from below;
I am from above.
You are of this world;
I am not of this world.[1]

These words could betoken a remote outsider or an Olympian differen-
tiating himself from mortals. But the evidence demands neither view.

Graham Greene has used Brighton Rock, a seaside sweetmeat in
which the same letters recur through the whole stick, as a symbol of
human nature. When we consider Jesus we recurrently face the juxta-
position, often the confusion, of two entirely contradictory views of individual and collective life. Deeply rooted in the linear view of history,
Mark and Matthew emphasise the impression (accepted by modern
writers from Schweitzer to Michael Grant[2]) that Jesus anticipated the
establishment of a kingdom in the here and now. The phrase used *ad
nauseam* in the modern United States, a twice-born Christian, springs
from the interpretation in linear terms of the sentence of Jesus:

Unless a man is born again (*anothen*)
he cannot see the kingdom of God.[3]

First one birth, then another. Yet the word *anothen* acquires apter
meaning when it is translated as 'from above', in the vertical, time-
despising sense.[4] Michael Grant: sees Jesus's repudiation of violence
as being motivated by an impatient anxiety to usher in the Kingdom of
God (in a temporal sense) so that 'even such a famous part of his teachings as his insistence on the abandonment of worldly hostilities was not
motivated by gentleness, or compassion, or pacifism, but by his con-
centration on the Kingdom and the all-important task of securing
admission to it'.[5]

This rejudaization of the gospel was already widespread in the early
years of the twentieth century; indeed, the process goes back to the
first century itself, and to such theological writers as the author of
Matthew. But the anti-Jewish persecutions of the Second World War
(themselves evidence of the decline of Christianity in the west) followed by the successful campaigns by Jewish settlers in Palestine
against the British and Arabs inspired a bay of books fostering a this-
worldly view of Jesus's mission. It is a corrective to return to the prayer
reportedly composed by Jesus which can claim to be the most frequently recited formula on earth. Although absent from Mark and

---

[1] John 8, 23: JB.
[2] Michael Grant: *Jesus*, London, 1977.
[3] John 3, 3.
[4] This is the primary sense given in the Lexicon of New Testament Greek: *from above,
from a higher place*. The *Jerusalem Bible* translates it 'unless a man is born from above'.
[5] Michael Grant: op.cit., p. 30.

John, and despite minor variations in the versions given by Matthew and Luke,[1] the Lord's Prayer contains ideas and words which must go back to Jesus. Take the first two. *Our father*: droned so often in church, or expounded to imply that Jesus taught a new, more intimate view of God, the emphasis is often placed on *father*, whereas it more reasonably falls on *our*. The good god is *our* father, thus distinguished from *their* father, whose kingdom exists already. Behind other phrases that seem homely to the point of dullness one finds further denial of the linear thesis. The petition, *Give us today our daily bread!* is as familiar as the pre-sliced loaf that bounces, wrapped, into western kitchens. The Jerusalem Bible admits in a note that the Greek adjective it translates as 'daily' is obscure: 'whatever the exact translation the sense is that we must ask God for the sustenance we need in this life but for no more – not for wealth and luxury.'

Since bread was to dominate the key mystery which Jesus instituted, we can profitably examine the original sentence. Transliterated from Matthew it reads:

ton 'arton 'emon ton 'epiousion dos 'emin semeron.

The eight words contain an intricate inner rhythm. The accusative masculine termination -*on*, for example, is repeated five times. The simplicity of seven of the eight words dramatises the eighth – '*epiousion* – which is found nowhere else in classical or New Testament Greek. Origen, an Egyptian Christian who lived between Alexandria and Palestine in the third century, testifies it was no longer current in his lifetime. The word is either a coinage by Jesus (which would confirm that he had more than a rustic command of Greek) or comes, as a translation of an Aramaic coinage, from a source known to Matthew and Luke.

What can it be understood to mean? Surely not daily: the notion of ephemerality would repeat the *semeron* of Matthew or the yet more explicit *to kath'emeran* of Luke. St Jerome, who translated the Greek scriptures into the Latin Vulgate, recognised the problem and rendered the passage in Matthew by the somewhat grotesque *panis super-substantialis*. For the petition to have the pith which characterises the sayings of Jesus it must embody antithetical balance, not tautological repetition. This can be found if we give the -*ousia* part of *epiousion* its Aristotelian meaning of essence, or real nature. The prayer would then contrast ephemerality, the world in which men and women seem to exist, with a break which belongs to a cosmos of reality.

Bread, as a link between the opposed worlds which dispute man's being, is not only central to this prayer but to the rite by which Jesus planned to keep the men and women of his kingdom conjoined to

[1] Matthew 6, 7–15; Luke 11, 1–4.

himself. Food is to the body what the sun is to the planet; cereals and
grapes derive with particular panache from the action of the sun. In the
recension of the Book of the Dead preserved in the British Museum
'beer and bread' were the reward of the justified.[1] A banquet symbolised the golden age of the future in Hebrew eschatology. Plato chose a
supper party, or symposium, for his master's discussion of love.

Yet the aroma of death has seeped into the love-feasts of Jesus
thanks to the synoptic link between the institution of bread and wine
and the Jewish Passover memorialising a massacre and the Crucifixion.
But John shows that in the opening stages of his mission Jesus was pro-
moting the love-feast as a means whereby his followers could achieve
identity with himself. The terms in which he did so were a major cause
of his losing Galilean support.

'The tragic thing was,' writes Michael Grant, an exponent of the
linear gospel, 'when his mission in Galilee began to encounter fatal opposition, that these privileged followers, too, began to fall away, as
John's Gospel records:

> When Jesus was giving instruction in Capernaum, many of his dis-
> ciples on hearing it exclaimed, "This is more than we can stomach.
> Why listen to this talk..." From that time on, many of his dis-
> ciples withdrew and no longer went about with him.'[2]

When we turn to Mr Grant's source, we find that what turned the
stomachs of the Galilean backsliders was not information about the
coming Kingdom but food metaphors as horrific to first-century Jews
as cartridges greased with animal fat to nineteenth-century Indian soldiers. Jesus was in closer touch with the Hellenistic than the Galilean
mind. The notion that the corn *was* Osiris was common to Egyptians
while a similar notion attached itself to Demeter and Persephone in
Hellas itself. But to understand the opposition to Jesus we should
reread John with provincial and conservatively educated Jews in mind:

> I tell you most truly,
> if you do not eat the flesh of the Son of Man
> and drink his blood,
> you have no life in you.
> Anyone who eats my flesh and drinks my blood,
> has eternal life,
> and I shall raise him up on the last day.

---

[1] Breasted: op. cit., p. 306: 'His righteous heart comes forth from the balances and he
has no sin in the sight of any god or goddess ... Let there be given to him the bread
and beer that come forth before Osiris-Unefer like the Followers of Horus.'
[2] Op. cit., p. 128. The privileged followers are, in the author's text, the disciples who
had replaced his family.

For my flesh is real food
and my blood is real drink.[1]

His metaphors were taken with the humourless rage that centuries later were to lead to the martyrdom of an Islamic saint who declared in ecstasy, 'I am the truth.'

From hostile literalists Jesus temporarily escaped, with those of his disciples whose alienation from traditional Judaism equalled his own, to the land east of the river where he had heard the Voice.

---

[1] John 6, 53–55: DS. Books have been written on the precise meaning of the phrase, 'the son of Man'. So far from being mysterious, it probably translates an Aramaic mode of referring to oneself. In this context it plainly refers to Jesus himself. The extended passage occupies vv. 26–58, John 6. 'He taught this doctrine in Capernaum.' It led, the following verses show, to the first schism.

CHAPTER FIFTEEN

The Bethany Pivot

The east bank of the Jordan valley rose to a plateau now covered with stubble after the spring harvest. Desert disputed the rest with clumps of forest trees. Shrubs still flowered in the dried-out wadis. The Greek cities scattered through the region did not tempt the Galileans with their range of diversions and their elegance of life. For these were the weeks in which Jesus demonstrated the mysteries of the new order which knowledge, effort and will could establish. Jerusalem the dangerous was far to the west beyond the shimmering valley and the white scoured mountains.

Then one morning early Jesus remarked that their friend in Bethany was sick. Shortly they would risk the return to Judaea. Then, 'He is sleeping.' Then, explicitly, 'He is dead. We must go now.' They left the valley as the sun lit the huts of Jericho. It was already hot. A haze hid the Dead Sea's stillness. Used to walking, even in summer, they reached the outskirts of the suburban village around noon, or a little later. Scruffy as bandits, the young men settled in the shade of a carob. Cool water trickled from behind black shade. Andrew reached up for a pod and ate it. Others were in haste to wash feet, then hands. The air was fresher than on the road but they had walked quickly and the village air stood still. Time seemed to cough, the unwobbling sun to have to come to rest forever.

Hêlios rules the month, not Pontius Pilate. The governor, like any Roman, came east to make money. His Jerusalem residence is the white turret. Brass glints against marble. When the time comes for him to crate his statues and couches, when the monotonous oars have carried him from Caesarea to Ostia and the imperial city, then retirement, he will not forget the climate in which he judged his victims. For the Levant is where the seaborne moisture meets, but does not mount or subdue, the dry ramparts that face the middle sea. And summer is the memorable season, but not the most pleasant. You can fry eggs on stones. Winds from across the Jordan bring dust that turns noon to midnight. Those with tender throats cower behind shutters, waiting for the autumn rainfall which stirs the new year. The pivot wobbles, the bleached grass pushes new green that banishes July and August

with their acts of violence. Cain must have slain his brother in August
and surely Abel stank before the next day's sunset.

Summer is a time for flight. Into cellars. Into arbours. Into closed
rooms. Into carts that lurch up tracks to hillside perches, to villages
hid by pines and soothed by cicadas. The young pagans step naked
onto beaches. Blinding sand meets sea, flesh meets flesh beneath
lucent water. At night the mounting to roofs, under stars, flesh tumes-
cent, the brain demanding. Yet the wine kept cool by day in springs
asks for bread, not rich men's sauces. Figs are plump. Dark spheres of
olives shine in briny jars.

The young men gaze over parched space, through trembling air, to
the glacier temple. From the tower a helmet sends a moment's dazzle.
Pilate is up from the coast. This is the month when fierce-eyed men
remember the temple's past destruction. Man's power seems to van-
quish God's. The profile of Tiberius stamps the coinage. Secluded
among his Capri pillars, the despot smirks, half in water, half on a
cushion laid across porphyry. Some darker emotion throbs the old
man's pustules. Caesar dreads Rome's brick vistas, the evergreen, the
smiling courtiers, the women with piled hair who delight in
bloodshed. Pilate's patron, Sejanus, has secured the dank dark corri-
dors, the dungeon apartments where ferns absorb the fetid water. So
Judas has heard from a travelled cousin.

He is the only disciple to think of power and potentates. The other
disciples stare, gnawing carob pods, towards the masonry massed
against eternity – or the end of eternity. Herod's temple is as old as
their fathers. And a thousand years before them, Solomon the Wise
had built a yet nobler temple. His architect from Tyre imported cedars
which lasted four centuries till, in a summer as hot as this, foreign soldiers fired them. The high roof of the entrance fell in a crash of lattice
windows. Flames shameless as whores had tongued the darkness. In a
tomb-dark cube, ten yards square, dwelt the unportrayed Something
that ruled the Hebrews: or the Someone. This ruler – its name was
hidden in the consonants of Yahweh – belonged to deserts, the night
and maleness, unlike the sun which most languages treated as female.
Yahweh had wrestled by night against a human being. *Let me go, for
day is breaking.* Like the moon, Yahweh's protection had a fickle cold-
ness. *Arise, Yahweh,* the tribes would chant, *let thine enemies be scattered, let them that hate thee flee from before thee.* But just as the moon
could inspire crime or madness, the Ark could draw peril on its behol-
ders. Perhaps no one had been entirely sorry when it perished. In the
foreign attack, or long before it. Who could be certain? The attackers
from the land of the Two Rivers melted the Bronze Sea, a cauldron
shouldered by lifelike bulls. Its sixteen thousand gallons had rushed
into the rock upholding David's city. The soldiers cast the metal into

portable ingots. But the temple had risen from its ashes on the same levelled platform. And now, throughout their lifetimes, this monster of marble had been adding, like a coral, colonnades and porticos.

The young men in tunics turned from the distant view to their standing leader. They recognised the signs of an impending action. Other men, not friendly, were watching him from other shadows. His eyes were on the temple, but in a hostile spirit. He now linked its inner function, they knew, with evil. But to Judas the temple remained one thing Romans could not rule; they even concurred in their exclusion, as gentiles, from its inner courtyard and high stepped altar. The other disciples, who spoke in the rough northern accent which Jerusalem laughed at, had been brought up to revere the temple. Yet *I can destroy the temple*, Jesus had said, *and in three days rebuild it*. He finds no serenity in dove blood or lamb flesh.

But their coming to Bethany is not for the temple. They have come to answer a summons from a woman. Despite the large house that will lodge them, despite the Egyptian physicians who have surely ridden down from the city, her brother has not recovered. Grieving reticence keeps them silent. In future they will have to seek their friend's memory past the stone his family will have shut against him. Stones are of two kinds: the flat stopper for a shaft-grave, or the round millstone that can be rolled to shut a hill grave. Stones keep the dead from polluting the village. They also stop wild animals defiling what may again be a man, if those who say there is a resurrection prove right, one day.

Thomas unwraps his flask and mixes its wine with water.

The marble of the temple darkens. The sun gives the summit a last bright halo. The birds make a final spurt of chatter.

A question hovers.

'How did he know Lazarus was dead?'

'We were dozing. He left us. He found out. Probably at night.'

'If he left us, I'd have seen. I sleep lightly.'

'Perhaps he travels in his sleep? We have seen greater wonders.'

'Egypt teaches drugs, along with other magic. If we were drugged, he'd have had time to make sure about the fever.'

'Anyway, it killed him.'

The first bat swoops under the carobs. They imagine the temple vespers where the priests are the actors. Descendants of Aaron, they sleep in during their turn of service. Over their drawers of fine linen, their long tight coats, narrow-sleeved, reach unshod feet. Each priest wears a decorated girdle, a lofty turban. The offering, a public gift, is to be renewed at nightfall forever. It will gorge the flame which flares, also forever, from the rough-stone altar. The lamps are lit, the incense ignited. A young male is led from the lamb-house and given a last drink from a golden bowl. He is gently led to where the place of slaughter has rings to hold him. He is without blemish. While one priest stands to catch his blood, a second strikes. The cadaver is placed on a special table. Its entrails are washed. Six priests carry the pieces to the blunt step pyramid. The thirsty stones of Yahweh's table catch the blood, still hot. Added to God's banquet are fine flour, the High Priest's baked offering, wine. Trumpets blare, psalms are chanted. All night the altar splutters under the stars. A controlled volcano, it asserts a ruler watching, demanding, judging. And in the morning there will be matins. This time the lights will be trimmed and the incense will follow, not precede, the severed throat and the spilt lifeblood.

'Now we shall enter the village. Keep a little from me.'

A stone mansion, sumptuous as any pagan villa by the sea, dominates Bethany's tangled alleys. Wooden structures matted with vines and lines of cypress partly hide its portico, averting envy.

As they approach, the light fades. A woman suddenly sorties. Her kohl-dark eyes are on their leader. *Sorties*: no less mannered a word would suit her step, so different from the hen-rush of a peasant woman.

The torches held by servants beat back the darkness. To their resinous aroma she adds her own scent, half of the tomb and half of the bedroom. Some sense of her shouted words reaches the disciples. Greek is spoken in all cities and pedlars of imported gewgaws tempt their mothers with back-door Greek. Her gestures, in any case, enforce her declamation. She prostrates herself grimly at their leader's feet, then rises to hurl a title. Son of Elias! Or is it Hêlios? Chrêstos: their leader's nickname. Yet a scolding tone in part belies her greeting. She turns and with fierce strides leads out of the village. The lighted windows, pale yellow oblongs, weaken behind them. The young men shiver. From afar, at Gerasium, in the Decapolis, they had glimpsed a theatre. On a high platform actors were miming women, haughty dames who strode on stilts and were more imposing than mortals. By the torchlight this woman could be an actor. Her face gleams green, then copper. Isis-horns ride her tresses. The young men halt at the wall which bounds the garden. By sunshine its stones would be lizard-flicked. Now they are cold and you half hear scorpions. Trees, too, are changed in torchlight. Some still as lances; olives without their double colour. Among the black shapes Jesus flickers like a candle, now caught, now lost, as he moves towards the hillside. The same with the woman. They can see that the tomb is upright, almost a cave-house. A round stone shuts it. One of them, Judas of the purse-strings, decides on bravado. He leaps the wall and rushes, arms outstretched, to dissuade their leader. But his power ebbs from him. As in nightmare. His tongue cannot utter.

Do they see what they think they see?

The tomb blinks open. It has looked inwards on the eternal silence. But as the lights catch lime's pallor they see Jesus by the low stone bed and its bundle of unmoving linen. He extends his hand. A phrase echoes. It is three times repeated. One of the disciples catches the Greek. He helps the others grasp, then lose, its meaning.

I become holy being initiate.

They catch, from new speech, *death* and *deathless*.

A sudden bellow. Heads straining to hear bristle like hedgehogs. Philip starts towards the village. Then shame halts his sandals. He, too, must look back, even if it harms him.

I have seen the dweller in distant silence: the eternal father.

The voice could be pushing through a wad of cheesecloth.

Now the extended hand commands a movement: a jerk, not a tremor. The horizontal parcel becomes a torso, struggling, first to sit up, then, rocking, to stand, leaning against the stone platform. The linen glides from him. He is tired, but living. He frees his face and, naked as a fisherman, embraces Jesus. It is a strange embrace. Men you distrust sometimes embrace in his manner. Or an uncertain bride trembling to her husband.

Risen is the new Osiris!

A group of girls, appearing from nowhere, clash cymbals and raise the joy-cries of a rustic wedding. One Galilean wonders why this day should have fatigued their Judaean treasurer more than the others. 'I have let him go too far,' he begins, till hurly-burly crushes his words. Aflame, without having drunk, all follow the joy-cries to the mansion. The woman has dropped her insistent way of walking. And, as though for an everyday fiesta, the dim-raftered rooms await them. The roof, set for feasting, is on a level with palm fronds and cypress. The couches are arranged in the coastal manner. Smiling servants ferry wine up the stone staircase.

I remember how, in Cana, once...

But was he dead? Sleeping? Acting?

Have they witnessed a resurrection, or a rite?

The wine, with the noise, confuses questions.

But the torchlight and tumult have attracted dark shapes and suspicious faces. The moths from Jerusalem: lawyers, temple servants, are in the public alley. But the Galileans watch the youth only. His head is wreathed; his pale brow runs with melting perfume. Next to him, his legs together, Jesus sits upright at the head of the diners. Excited villagers have sometimes hailed him as like King David; he is closer to the Egyptian with the clover features. But the wine blurs legend with legend, Osiris with Mithras, Moses with Attis.

The freed cadaver smiles to the magician who revived him.

'Chrêstos, what of Mithras? He, too, fights our war between light and darkness. The sun behind the sun is his protector. His friends baptise. There are no women in his rituals.'

'"I came to destroy the works of the female!"? I did not mean, the absence of women. I meant, in the kingdom, no male, no female.'

'And they have their banquet in the time of Leo.'

'And we dream of a world without the temple.'

The talk is beyond the interest of the others, but Judas hears this.

'But is it true, about the bull-bath?'

This intrigues Thomas.

'You tell us, Lazarus.'

'On nights as happy as this they huddle beneath interwoven metal. They hear the bull's hooves slithering above their heads. They squint up and see the soles of the armed priest. His sword lunges at the heaving stomach, the warm entrails behind the short pelt. The blood hisses and gushes through the openings. The men of Mithras glisten in hot purple.'

Their leader reverts to Aramaic.

'But this is my blood.'

He holds out a goblet and a servant refills it. He offers the first sip to Lazarus, and then hands it to the others. He reaches for a crisp loaf, a cartwheel baked that dawn in the earth oven, and divides it. To each a fragment.

'And this is my body.'

While the cup is still passing, a servant adds dishes to the table: figs, the seeds of pomegranates, boiled eggs, sliced cucumbers and olives. Soon, all sleep, where they fall, exhausted. Only Jesus stares beyond the cypresses and the guttering torches at the constellations. He once said, foxes have lairs, birds have nests: I have nowhere to lay my head. He gazes at the sky as if there he had property.

But in the morning Peter has an upset stomach. Returning with washed hands he hears the urgent tones of Judas.

'They saw everything and went before dawn to the city. I warned you.'

'They want to kill me? But even their law requires a reason. And have I done good or evil?'

'You healed: but your forgiveness of sins was blasphemous.'

'I took from them the burden of guilt.'

'You know the penalty?'

'Stoning from a wall: I know it.'

'I'm guessing at their first intentions, when they saw you as a fair-ground magician. Now they say you have imported the foul tomb magic. They say it, not I.'

'My actions lead away from graveyard places. The man who knows comes out of the death-place living. You saw, Judas.'

'I saw, Chrêstos. But the Mithraists, too, have places of mock-entombment.'

'And now?'

'They will seek to kill you, but not by stoning. They will choose some way that kills your fame, some way that pollutes you.'

John's gospel pivots on what happened at Bethany. 'From that day they were determined to kill him.' These sinister words conclude the episode.[1]

Yet neither the church nor secular writers seem[2] to have accepted John's sequence of motivation and effect. It is easy to account for ecclesiastical caution. John's gospel, unlike the other three, was early criticised for gnostic tendencies. Not that this prevented its inclusion in the canon.[3] Again, particularly in recent centuries, the church has been cautious over miracles and what is said to have happened at Bethany is to other miracles what Mount Everest is to Ben Nevis. In Jewish popular belief the soul was thought to stay close to the body for no more than three days. The assertion that Lazarus had lain in the tomb for four days implies the certainty of corruption. Jesus apparently brings back to life someone completely dead.

Since John omits parables of words, some critics have taken the raising of Lazarus as an allegory, prefiguring the greater resurrection shortly to take place.[4] Certainly it has an evident link with the parable, itself possessing unique features, of Dives and Lazarus.[5] For while *dives* is simply the Latin for rich man, Lazarus is the Greek form of Eliezer, and thus the only instance of a proper name appearing in a parable. In his account of the miracle, John tells us that Jesus loved Lazarus and wept for him: the one display of personal emotion recorded of Jesus.

Then, in 1958, new evidence made the story something more than

---

[1] John 11,53.

[2] *Seem*: a necessary caution. More than sixty thousand works on Jesus are said to have been published in the nineteenth century alone.

[3] John appears in the Codex Sinaiticus, our earliest book version of the New Testament. It also figures in the Muratorian Fragment, a Latin list of the New Testament canon compiled around AD 200.

[4] George Milligan (*The New Testament Documents*, London, 1913: p. 157) refers to 'the view that the Gospel is nothing but a thorough-going allegory, in which its writer deliberately inserted invented situations and composed speeches in order to bring home to men's minds more fully the ideal conception of the Christ that had taken possession of him'.

[5] Luke 16, 19–31.

an event peculiar to John. Morton Smith, the American scholar already referred to in the context of Jesus's wonders, was working on monastic detritus at Mar Saba, a dozen miles east of Jerusalem, when he found indications that Mark, the earliest and most ruggedly factual of the gospels, had at one time contained the story. The monastery of Mar Saba, a terraced group of white buildings in saffron desert, dated from the fifth century. At that time Palestine was as devoted to the religious life as Egypt itself. And even after the coming of Islam in the seventh century Mar Saba's Greek monks continued much as before. Their book collection consisted largely of pietistic works, many of which were destroyed in an eighteenth century fire. Remaining items of value had then been transferred to the safety of Ottoman Jerusalem. Smith, gleaning the scant remains, made an exciting find. A seventeenth century printed edition of the letters of a minor church father incorporated in its cardboard binding the manuscript of a Greek letter. This manuscript itself was dated by the palaeographers Smith consulted to no earlier than the late seventeenth century, but, like much monastic literature, the document was a calligraphic sampler. That is, a monk had been set to copy it, either to replace an older copy in bad repair or to keep him from mischief. But the resulting manuscript seemed to be the copy of an original third-century letter written by Clement of Alexandria to Theodore, an otherwise unknown Palestinian correspondent. Clement wrote a distinctive Greek. Scholars can distinguish it from that of other Alexandrians as confidently as students of English literature could distinguish a letter by Dr Samuel Johnson from one by Charlotte Brontë.

Clement was replying to an inquiry from Theodore about a fuller version of Mark which the Alexandrian church showed only to advanced Christians: on the principle, in Clement's words, that 'not all things are to be said to all men'. Theodore wanted information on this secret gospel since he was controverting a sect which taught that spiritual liberation could be achieved through the deliberate defiance of traditional norms of behaviour. Such defiance could take the form of extreme asceticism – or extreme indulgence. Clement's letter (considered genuine by most of the authorities whom Smith consulted) denied that the 'more spiritual gospel for the use of those who were being perfected' justified libertine practices. To prove this, Clement copied out for Theodore the incident in the fuller version of Mark which the libertines had claimed as supporting their view. What Clement quoted was evidently John's story, but told in the terse, non-literary style of Mark.

There are minor differences. Clement's Mark has only one woman. This is not surprising, as the duplication of figures is an artistic device common in the New Testament. Nor is it important, since John confirms the pre-eminence of Mary, when he refers to the Jews having come to condole with her.[1] Mark's Mary addresses Jesus as 'Son of David', which fits the second gospel's view of Jesus. Jesus thereupon accompanies her to the garden, some way from the house, and rolling aside the stone himself, enters the tomb. He extends his hand to the young man, whom Mark does not name, and raises him. The youth is said to love Jesus – not the other way round – and asks to be with him. They then return to the young man's house.

Besides padding the story with a theological discourse, John gives more details. He identifies the man as 'Lazarus, our friend'; Jesus somehow knows in advance that Lazarus has fallen asleep. We are told how long Lazarus has been in the tomb and that Bethany is roughly two miles from Jerusalem. John, who stresses that Jesus loves the youth and weeps for him, orders others to move the stone and, after talking to God, utters a loud cry. The dead man walks from the tomb, his face still swaddled.

What the stories share is more important. Both preface their accounts with the information that Jesus and his disciples had been walking east of the Jordan as well as in Judaea. Both set the story in Bethany.[2] Both focus on the woman whose brother has died and who prostrates herself to Jesus. The climax of both stories is the emergence of the corpse.

This minimal residue has momentous implications for those who believe that the gospels contain some species of historical truth. The story can no longer be dismissed as a mere allegory of Jesus's own resurrection. If the Mar Saba letter is genuine, Peter's confidant, Mark, confirms the recollection of a man who had been young in the last days of Tiberius.

The survival of the episode in two sources compels us to consider its possible factual basis and meaning. The possible answers are restricted.

The story could be a pious fiction whose picturesque value inspired Caravaggio and other painters. The alleged miracles of the infant Alexander provided similar inspiration to Greco-Roman painters.

Or, if we believe in a god that interrupts the laws of nature, the raising of Lazarus could be a more spectacular version of Elijah's raising of the widow's son.[3] A young man's circulation and nerve impulses have ceased; the consequences of cellular dissolution have begun to show themselves in stench: Jesus intervenes to reflood the brain and add an extra span to his friend's existence.

[1] John 11,31.
[2] In its modern Arabic name of Al-Azariyah, the initial of Lazarus has been displaced into the article, *al-*.
[3] 1 Kings 17, 17–24.

Or, in a third interpretation which seems to me the more likely, strange events did take place at Bethany but were misunderstood by those who witnessed them. If we see the incident in the garden in the context of the mystery cults prevalent in the first-century Levant, we have an explanation which demands neither miracle nor *pia fraus*.

Egyptian mysteries centred on Osiris, the god of the dead whom the Old Kingdom had identified with the deceased king. But the mystery associated with the god – killed by his brother Set and restored to life by Isis and Horus – had long been democratised. As early as the eighteenth Dynasty the papyrus of Ani, a major recension of the Egyptian Book of the Dead, identifies Ani, an ecclesiastical official, with the immortal Osiris. By the time of Jesus any individual could aspire to identity with Osiris after death if he had lived virtuously and could afford the funerary rituals required. Our modern phrase, the late so-and-so, had its equivalent in the term 'the Osiris so-and-so'. During his lifetime a man could ease his future passage by initiation. A Greek scholar has established that an individual 'could only benefit from an initiation thanks to the ordeal of a simulated death'.[1] This ordeal meant, in other words, that a living person underwent a mock entombment and lay for a certain period of time in the condition of a corpse.

If the resurrection witnessed at Bethany was part of a simulated death, it leaves the important question: who was the initiate?

Lazarus is one of the two persons in the New Testament whom Jesus is said to love and the one person who arouses a physical emotion, that of tears. John is the source for both these claims, the second of which involves himself as the beloved disciple and author of the gospel.[2] Mark's gospel passes over both loves in clamorous silence. In the expanded text, as we have seen, Mark makes the young man love Jesus.

The apostolic age was immune to neither faction nor jealousy. The climax of Jesus's mission contained much to make Peter resentful, or ashamed. The beloved disciple was to get Peter admitted to the High Priest's house.[3] Once inside, Peter was to deny Jesus thrice while by contrast John alone of the male disciples would follow him to Golgotha. John, not Peter, was to be charged with the care of Mary.

A plausible explanation is that Lazarus and the author of the fourth gospel were one and the same person. Both are Judaeans. Both are young. The disciple who on an impulse switched allegiance from the Baptist to Jesus was of a temperament to practise mysteries and understand their meaning.

There would then remain a problem of names. How does Lazarus

[1] S.Mayassis: *Mystères et Initiations de l'Egypte Ancienne*, Athens, 1957.
[2] Cf. John 19, 26 & 21, vv. 20 & 24.
[3] John 18, 15–16.

become John? One answer is that conversion is often signalled by a
name-change. The boxer Muhammad Ali was once Cassius Clay; Al
Hassan Ibn Muhammad Al Wezaz Al Fasi became Leo Africanus
when he was baptised by Pope Leo X. The process often embodies a
compliment. When T.E. Lawrence changed surnames for the second
time, he paid a filial compliment to Bernard and Charlotte by calling
himself Shaw. If the young Lazarus (already using a Greek form of the
Hebrew Eliezer) renamed himself John after the Baptist, in the days of
his discipleship, the name could have stuck and would help to explain
the profusion of Johns in the circle of Jesus's disciples. Lazarus was
probably rich as well as young. If so, Jesus showed his particular
humour in naming the poor man of his parable after his Bethany
friend.

   That the Jerusalem Jews watched the events at Bethany with mounting hostility is not surprising. The clergy could accept with philosophic resignation the involvement of Galileans in a heterodox
movement. They would violently condemn a Judaean youth who had
connections with the High Priest's household and yet took part in
necromantic rites. If the author of the gospel was the same youth who
staggered hungry and exalted from the tomb, this could explain the
later promptness of his flight, with Mary, out of Palestine, when all
seemed over.

CHAPTER SIXTEEN

A Summer Passion

Awkward details, events it would have been more convenient to omit, these are the gems of authenticity. A constellation of such indicates that Jesus's career reached its climax in summer.

Personal recollection underlies John's judgment that the road to Golgotha began at Bethany. Yet, without such personal knowledge, Mark and Matthew begin their accounts of the fatal last week with a puzzling incident set in the vicinity of the same small village. Jesus sleeps the last Sunday night of his life in Bethany. 'In the morning, on his way back to the city, he felt hungry. Noticing a fig tree by the road side, he went up to it but found nothing on it but leaves. And he said to it: "May you be fruitless to eternity!" And immediately the fig tree withered.'[1] Mark's version is similar; several manuscripts add the gloss, intelligible in the context, that it was not the season for figs.

The incident faced the two synoptics who used it to introduce Holy Week with an awkward problem. By the time they were writing it had become accepted teaching to link the drama of the passion with the Jewish passover. This annual feast always fell in the spring month of Nisan. Yet Jesus curses a summer-fruiting tree for not bearing fruit in early spring. His unreasonable anger seems to have inspired one twentieth-century writer with distaste for Jesus.[2] The first-century Luke discreetly buried the material in a parable.[3]

But Jesus is tiredly hungry rather than capriciously angry if we picture the events as happening not in spring but in Ab, the month corresponding to July/August. Then ripe figs load the trees from Alexandria to Cyprus. If we first regard the incident as genuine and then relocate it with the last week of Jesus's life to high summer, we admittedly forfeit the adherence of a gospel event to an old Testament pattern. But such correspondences are all too often contrived. The

---

[1] Matthew 21, 18–19: DS. Mark's version of the story comes in chapter 11, 12–14.
[2] 'The Gospel of St Mark ought to be explained, it is the question of the character of Christ – old hat perhaps. But when you come to look into him, was he not a thoroughly nasty man? How can one excuse the barren fig-tree?' *The Letters of J. R. Ackerley*, ed. Neville Braybrooke: to Francis King, 11.10.1964.
[3] Luke 13, 6–9.

cursing of the fig tree is immediately preceded by Matthew's account
of the entry into Jerusalem. There his eagerness to establish a link
between what Jesus does and what Matthew understood (wrongly) an
Old Testament prophet to have predicted makes him have Jesus ride
not one animal, but two: a feat difficult for a circus performer.[1] By
discarding the Old Testament link we gain in probability. The story
now makes sense. After the long walk the day before, the strain of the
nocturnal rite, and the threatening hostility of the Jews, the tree which
is barren when it should be fruitful suggests itself as a symbol of the
system which, Jesus sees now if he had not seen before, is out to
destroy him. High summer also consorts with other details that have
survived into the passion story. On the wooded slopes of the Mount of
Olives, on the night of his arrest, a young man escapes the police. '(He)
had nothing on,' Mark tells us in an episode to which we shall revert,
'but a linen cloth. They caught hold of him, but he left the cloth in
their hands and ran away naked.'[2] Such a light garment hardly fits the
overcoat chill of early spring. The heat of Ab, and its historical associ-
ations, could exacerbate tempers to a lynching mood. For August was
linked in the popular mind with the destruction of Solomon's temple,
accomplished on the 9th of Ab. The recurrent charge that Jesus had
threatened to destroy the temple of Herod could stir nationalist
hysteria among the people at this time more than at passover, which
celebrated a victory. Those who earned their living from the temple
and those who upheld the law which ordained its rituals were already
against him.

---

[1] Matthew misunderstands the Hebrew parallelism used by Zechariah (9,9): 'he rides
on a donkey and on a colt, the foal of a beast of burden'; the prophet is describing one
animal but Matthew, who was obviously not present, has the disciples bringing two
animals and making Jesus mount on both at once. The Gospel of Thomas (v.47) has
Jesus cite the riding of two animals as an instance, like stretching two bows, of impossi-
bility.
[2] Mark 14, 51–52: JB.

Part Two

THE TRAP IS SPRUNG

CHAPTER SEVENTEEN

Entry To The Dangerous City

In the rest of the Hellenistic world Jesus would have had no cause to feel anxiety over his modes of healing and his symbolic language. Yet in Palestine itself, like the enemies of the Holy Inquisition or twentieth-century police states, Jesus was aware of the suspicions his way of life could stir in others. His outburst against the holy city in the last days of his life – 'Jerusalem, Jerusalem, that kill the prophets and stone those that are sent to you!' – is likely to be genuine. It is not only found in identical form in Matthew and Luke[1] but is a wild exaggeration. As such it seems the utterance of a foreigner to whom Jerusalem seems a symbol of intransigence rather than a physical metropolis.

Like others who have lived close to people less intelligent than themselves, Jesus could read the signs of change in Judas, the most practical of his companions. Judas exerts, from the pious, faceless names recorded in the gospels, the mesmeric attraction of the man singled out. His traitorous role has given him the antagonistic glamour Milton could not sponge from his portrait of Satan. We know nothing of what drew Judas to join Jesus in the first place. His surname, Iscariot, has been variously explained. It was traditionally but unconvincingly derived from 'ish Keriyoth', a place in Judaea. Others have argued with some plausibility that Iscariot is a corruption of *sicarius*, a Latin word with the connotations of terrorist.[2] An innovator like Jesus might well have found recruits among the already unsettled: misfits intrinsically drawn to religion or those whose dissatisfaction with the state of the world drew them to political violence. The conversion of a terrorist to the universalism of Jesus may have come through despair at the impotence of nationalist action. Abandonment of political hope may have brought him the species of rapturous happiness whose origin William James was to trace to a radical pessimism.[3] In deciding to abandon Jesus to his heterodox road, or by a dramatic action to force him back towards Jewish orthodoxy, the Judas of the last phase may

---

[1] Matthew 23, 37; Luke 13, 34.
[2] Hyam Maccoby: *Revolution in Judaea*, London, 1973: p. 264.
[3] William James: *The Varieties of Religious Experience, A Study in Human Nature*, New York, 1969: p. 136.

have known the relief which some twentieth-century communists seem to have found in leaving the Party to return to the Church. A time-travelling psychologist would almost certainly have classified Judas as a neurotic predisposed to abrupt mood-swings.

Yet we may agree with Schweitzer: the important thing about Judas, historically, is not why he betrayed, but what.[1] The treachery can hardly have been limited only to informing the authorities where Jesus could be conveniently arrested. The Sanhedrin would have had cheaper ways of securing such information. What the religious leaders needed was a charge which could arouse general indignation while cloaking their own need to dispose of a menace to their incomes and influence. This charge Schweitzer took to be the messianic secret accurately uncovered by Peter and disclosed by him to the other disciples. It seems more reasonable to suppose that Judas could confirm the charge that necromancy, or a magical operation involving a corpse, had been central to the miracle at Bethany. The raising of Lazarus, which we may assume to have become more spectacular with each retelling, made threats to destroy and rebuild the temple politically dangerous. The high priests would take seriously the malice behind this claim while a Roman governor, whatever his views, could recognise the danger of such boasts to eastern crowds whose faith in the miracle-worker was at white heat.[2] What Judas could sell for thirty pieces of silver was detailed confirmation of what Jesus had done in the garden at Bethany.

Since there was no time in the last hectic days for Jesus to confide his state of mind to his disciples, the gospel-writers conjectured his motives for entering the city he distrusted and his sentiments as he did so.

John once again gives the most solid material for reasonable guesswork. The event at Bethany, his young disciple's emergence from a simulated death, posed to a first-century mind the possibility that what had been done in simulacrum could next be done in fact. The entombment could have gone wrong. Instead, Lazarus had come out of the ordeal alive and believing. The disciples had their faith confirmed while admiring crowds gaped for new wonders. The effect on Jesus, exhausted by physical effort and psychic strain, must have been as radical as John depicts it. It decided him to risk the city he believed murderous to those with a divine mandate, to affirm, even there, the

---

[1] 'For a hundred and fifty years the question has been historically discussed why Judas betrayed his Master. That the main question for history was *what he betrayed* was suspected by few.' Schweitzer: op.cit., p. 394.
[2] Lord Kitchener's alleged desecration of the Mahdi's skull after the victory of Omdurman was a similar response to a 'native' fanaticism to whose logic the Englishman was immune but of whose subjective power he was aware.

kingdom which could be entered by right knowledge here and now. Later accounts inevitably enlarge his entry to a triumph. John's account is the tersest. If we exclude the scriptural proof texts (almost certainly supplied by later editors) his account focuses on what occasioned the uproar. 'The crowd of people who had seen him when he called Lazarus from the tomb and raised him from the dead were giving their eyewitness accounts. This brought the common people out to meet him, as they had heard he had worked this wonder.'[1] Rumour moves fast in the east and on this occasion had short distance to travel. The leafy village of Mary and her brother could be seen, down below the eastern ramparts, marking the turn in the road which spiralled down to Jericho and the Jordan rift. A credulous age believes the fantastic quickly but its flaring confidence may as quickly go off the boil.

The common people surge from the lanes to greet him with palm fronds, even in summer green with life. The Pharisees share a sense of temporary impotence. 'There is nothing to be done. Everyone is running after the impostor.' Jesus enters the city by an everyday method. 'He found a young donkey and mounted it.'[2]

Once within the walls, Jesus hears less hubbub. The first serious inquirers, a group of Greeks, want to meet him. Converts to monotheism, they approach him through Philip who consults that other lakeside disciple with a Hellenic name, Andrew. They in turn approach Jesus, who in John's account addresses them in gnomic language, which was probably what they had come to hear. A striking passage is incorrect horticulturally but in the context of the Osiris cult symbolically true:

> Unless a wheat grain falls to earth and dies, it remains but a single grain; but if it dies, it yields a rich harvest.[3]

It was common practice in Egypt for rough outlines in red ink to depict Osiris on a cloth stetched over a wooden frame, itself laid on top of a rush bed. The silhouette of the god was smeared with a compost

[1] The synoptics have far less precise motivation. Mark has Jesus hailed as coming in the name of the Davidic kingdom; Matthew's onlookers speak of a prophet from Nazareth in Galilee; Luke uses the vague phrase, 'the coming one, the king in the name of the Lord'.

[2] John 12,14. Their absence from the scene is clearly signalled by the synoptics. Matthew, as we have seen, goes to great pains to have Jesus ride two animals at once. His crowds strew their cloaks in the road and cut branches from unspecified trees. Mark also has cloaks but, instead of branches, *stidades*, a Greek word which could be translated greenery or straw. Luke makes no attempt to identify the vegetation and has garments only. But they compensate for this imprecision by the complexity of their accounts of how Jesus arranges his mount, exotic to a modern reader but to the first century as normal as a taxi.

[3] John 12, 24: DS.

containing seeds of barley. When the seeds had sprouted a few inches they were reaped as symbols of the resurrection of the corn-god. Even in the tomb life was never absent.

John may have expanded the more dithyrambic passages which he sets in this interval; he may have placed some of them out of sequence. Yet the passages fit the clash of exaltation and menace which Jesus felt. He has been accepted by the common people but senses the opposition, even hatred, of their betters. Confidence in himself and his heavenly patron are balanced by a sense of the power of evil. He identifies himself with light and the enemy with darkness. The ultimate defeat of the enemy is sure: his own anguish not less so.

The Greeks witness a mood of self-communing:

Shall I ask my father to save me from this crisis?
It is for this that I came into the world.

And a few moments later:

Now is this world on trial:
now the *archon* of this world is about to be banished.

Only thereafter does he make explicit the full meaning of his presence:

Only for a little longer is the light among you.
Live while you have the light
So that the dark does not seize you.
The walker in darkness does not see where he is going.
While you have the light
believe in the light
and you will become sons of light.[1]

Here at the climax of his mission Jesus uses the timeless language of the gnostics. It is replete with the ambiguity inherent in most poetry. Is the light Jesus only – or the span of human existence? Light (and the sun) oppose darkness and the fickle moon: his god stands against the ruler of this world. Yahweh only – or all social systems?

Judas had already begun to reject Jesus just as most Galileans had rejected him. These disquisitions can only have confirmed his resolution. Jesus says nothing of a special role for one people, exempts no law or religious institution from the banishment which is to be the fate of this world's *archon*. To Greeks loosely converted to the monotheistic aspects of Judaism, these ideas made sense. But the mystical majesty in which he rephrased the universalism of the Therapeutae would have outraged the Essenes.

Κἀγὼ ἐὰν ὑψωθῶ ἐκ τῆς γῆς,

[1] John 12, 27–36: DS.

Πάντας ἑλκύδω πρὸς ἐμαυτόν

The Jerusalem Bible translates these words.

And when I am lifted up from the earth,
I shall draw all men to myself.[1]

The literal translation would be:

And I, if I am exalted from the earth,
Will draw all men to me.

A well-attested variant[2] for 'all men' reads 'all things', 'the all', giving an even more gnostic emphasis to his words.

On the lips of this enigmatic man, in the aftermath of his greatest miracle, with the applause of the crowds in his ears, these words could assimilate Jesus to the sun whose inner power inclines all vegetation to itself. But it was inevitable, in the context of what was about to happen, what, writing two generations later, John intrudes: 'By these words he designated the kind of death he was to die.'

[1] John 12, 32.
[2] i.e. πάντά, which is found in a Greek papyrus from about AD 200, the original text of the fourth-century Codex Sinaiticus, the sixth-century Codex Bezae, the Old Latin, the Vulgate and other versions.

CHAPTER EIGHTEEN

Betrayal

In political betrayals the paymaster is usually more important than the traitor.

Under the Roman occupation of Judaea, the clergy, in particular the High Priest, filled a role which anticipated in scope, and limits, that of the various religious leaders in the Ottoman empire.[1] Caiaphas, the High Priest, and his father-in-law, the former High Priest Annas, enjoyed prestige and wealth but knew that both could be removed if they failed to play their part in the imperial design.

These were the dignitaries whom Judas secretly contacted at some moment between Jesus's entry into Jerusalem and his last meal with his disciples. It may have been as early as Monday, when the other disciples were sleeping off the exertions of the recent days.

Mark, followed by Matthew, gives a matter of fact account of the betrayal:

> And Judas Iscariot, one of the twelve, went to the high priests to discuss betraying him to them. They jumped at the idea and undertook to reward him. He next sought how most conveniently to hand him over.[2]

Mark's source was doubtless as prejudiced against Judaeans, seeing them as mercenary and tricky, as Judaeans were against the northerners whose accents they laughed at and whose lack of religious learning they despised. Judas needed no supernatural encouragement to betray. Luke and John explain the betrayal in terms of Satanic persuasion. This could have a symbolic truth unintended by the gospel-writers if Jesus's antagonist in the wilderness was one aspect of Yahweh. For Judas probably saw his action as a reconciliation with the god of his youth, not as a betrayal of the new. If so, the satisfaction was to be abstract and short-lived. His experience of the difference between the calculating priests and the man on whose words he had once soared into the heavens was to shatter his existence.

[1] In Cyprus the Archbishop of the Orthodox Church was recognised by the Turks as leader of the Greeks in temporal as well as religious affairs. But if his community caused the Sultan trouble he could forfeit his goods, even his life.

[2] Mark 14, 10–11: DS.

When it comes to the motives of the priests, the gospels are less simple-minded. Mark assumes the priests had decided to kill Jesus by the time his group left Bethany. Although Mark links the village with an incident of a woman anointing Jesus at the house of a leper, he indirectly confirms John's narrative. Mark sees the priests as preoccupied with preventing a popular disturbance and hence devising means to take Jesus by stealth. Matthew adds that the plot was mooted in the palace of Caiaphas. Luke stresses the plotters' fear of the people.

But important questions are left unanswered. Why, in fact, did Caiaphas and his underlings wish to get rid of Jesus? What means did they envisage? For what specific role was Judas paid?

No one in the priestly circle feared that Jesus was the messiah, though some must have wondered if he thought himself a claimant. Those Jews who awaited the predicted deliverer knew that he had to be of the house of David and would be anointed by a prophet. (Neither the Sadducees nor the zealots expected a messiah.) Joseph, Mary's husband, may, like many others, have claimed descent from David. But the gospels indicate that even the paternity of Jesus, let alone Davidic antecedents, fell under doubt. The accusation against him that he was a 'glutton and drunkard' involved, to contemporaries, the charge that he was a bastard.[1]

Apart from their understandable objection to his attacks on themselves, the priests were alarmed that an agitation which could turn to riot might imperil their accommodation with Roman power. The linchpin of this power was the Antonia fortress, brooding above the temple. Jesus might be no intentional troublemaker but his teachings, half understood, could work up mobs he would be unable to control. Such fears were realistic. Nationalist hysteria was to convulse Jewish Palestine in the 60s. Discontent linked to implausible dreams of divine intervention were to play into the hands of zealots, themselves prepared to risk armed revolt against the legions. 'There was no evil that did not stem from them and from which the people were affected beyond description: wars, from the unceasing violence of which none was spared; loss of friends who might have lightened our sufferings; large-scale brigandage; the murder of important persons – it was all done on the pretext of the common good; but, in reality, it was motivated by personal gain.'[2] So Josephus, who was to side with the Romans. But the inevitable response of a Rome defied was to depopulate Jerusalem and leave the temple a ruin. The priests were never to recover their

---

[1] Ethelbert Stauffer: *Jesus and His Story*, New York, 1959: p. 201. Professor Stauffer quotes the good form of Talmudic time: if a bastard led a life pleasing to God, his illegitimacy should go unremarked; but if the *mamzer* became an apostate, his illegitimate birth should be spoken of publicly and unsparingly.

[2] *Antiquities*, xviii: 6–8.

commanding role in Jewish life. The ease with which the temple was replaced by congregational worship shows that, covertly at least, a majority of Jews found sacrifice a meaningless burden.

Caiaphas and his intimates were moved by such pragmatic considerations. But other members of the Sanhedrin were doubtless as sincere as the priests who advised Agamemnon to slaughter Iphigenia so as to obtain a fair wind for Troy. Time-servers and reactionary idealists could, for different motives, feel alarm at the episode in Bethany. Jesus already had the reputation of a miracle-worker. His latest feat, the talk of the holy city, made popular uproar only too probable. It aroused horror in those who suspected necromantic rites.

The plans to neutralise Jesus – such a periphrasis suits the context – were a tribute to his commanding personality. Unlike Stephen, he could not be disposed of by a subsidised lynching. A judicial action remained a theoretical alternative. Many scholars dispute the statement attributed to the Jews (in John's account) that 'it is not lawful for us to put any man to death'. But the enemies of Jesus were as concerned to destroy his power as to end his life. A conviction for blasphemy, for falsely claiming to be a prophet, could have been followed by ritual stoning. (The Romans seem to have condoned the lynching of gentiles who strayed beyond a certain point in the temple.) This would have silenced his lips. But like other martyrs he could have reigned more terribly from the tomb. What was needed was a solution which would discredit Jesus among the simple. Conveniently, the Roman method of executing political criminals could do precisely that, and, if the Romans were involved, any opprobrium would be lifted from priestly shoulders.

A Jewish historian has described crucifixion, the punishment introduced to Palestine by Varus, the Roman legate to Syria, as 'the most barbarous form of punishment ever invented'. Hyam Maccoby traces its origins to a form of human sacrifice supposed to fertilise the earth; the practice was of ultimately middle eastern origin, since it derived through the Carthaginians from Phoenician worshippers of Tammuz. 'To the Jews,' Maccoby writes, 'crucifixion was a particularly loathsome and horrifying form of inhumanity.'[1] He is right in implying that it was the nightmare fate which every zealot had to take account of when embarking on his violent career. But he and other twentieth-century writers are incorrect in implying that it had never been used by Jews. The seven sons of Saul seem to have been crucified as an expiatory sacrifice to Yahweh. David, perplexed by a three-year famine, interrogated the god as to the reasons for this disaster. It was revealed to him that there was a blood-guilt on Israel because Saul, David's pre-

[1] Hyam Maccoby: *Revolution in Judaea, Jesus and the Jewish Resistance*, London, 1973: p. 45.

decessor as king, had executed the Gibeonites. Before the fertility of the land could be restored, these deaths had to be expiated. Centuries later, Alexander Jannaeus (BC 104–78), the grandson of Judas Maccabaeus, defeated a rival faction of Jews and took them as prisoners with him to Jerusalem. 'There within the city, at least according to the account of Josephus, while he along with his mistress gave himself up to debauchery, he had somewhere around eight hundred of the prisoners crucified in his presence, and while they were yet alive caused their wives and children to be slain before their eyes.'[1]

As a form of execution crucifixion was especially used when (in Maccoby's words) 'the criminal was considered deserving of the utmost contempt and humiliation'. Jewish theory added a spiritual sting to its extended agonies: a curse heavy enough to pollute the land if the victim remained on the tree overnight.[2]

The problem was thus to arrest Jesus without popular protest or religious fuss, to have him sentenced and executed under Roman law. Only in that way might his execution and disposal put a final stop to his reputation and power.

Clearly Judas could fill more than one function and about several there is no mystery. He could obviate a hue and cry by designating time and place. The familiar sight of their treasurer, till then unsuspected, could prevent the disciples from rallying with collective violence to an attack on their leader. And more important yet, he could give the support of an eye-witness to some of the charges the clergy were preparing to bring against Jesus.[3] But one curious detail in the oldest account of the planned arrest suggests that Judas may have had more to offer: information that Jesus would be conducting another secret rite in the nocturnal garden. Peter seems to have told Mark that a half-naked young man was with Jesus as the soldiers arrived with staves and torches to arrest him.[4] Mark was to hazard no explanation, only to describe the manner in which the youth escaped.

So much for the role of Judas. Once they had Jesus under restraint, the priestly gerontocracy had the problem of convincing the Romans

---

[1] Schürer: op.cit., Vol. 1, p. 40.
[2] Deut. 21, 22–23. Immediately after prescribing stoning for a rebellious or stubborn son, the legislator writes: 'If a man guilty of a capital offence is put to death and you hang him on a tree, his body must not remain on the tree overnight; you must bury him the same day, for one who has been hanged is accursed of God, and you must not defile the land that Yahweh your God gives you for an inheritance.'
[3] According to the Talmudic account in Talbab, Sanhedrin 43a, the charge for which Jesus was executed was that he practised sorcery and enticed Israel to apostasy.
[4] 'A lad who followed him wore nothing but a *linen cloth* on his naked body; they seized him but he let slip the cloth and escaped them naked.' Mark 14, 50–52: DS. The word for a linen cloth – *sindona* – is the same word used by the synoptics for the shroud in which Jesus was to be interred.

that what was bad for the temple was also bad for Rome. Although Jesus might seem a person of less importance to Roman authority than his later disciple, Paul of Tarsus – whose preaching career enjoyed extension thanks to his legal status as a Roman citizen – the priests must be prudent. They had already tried to trap Jesus into advising Jews not to pay tribute to the emperor. He had escaped the trap by asking for a Roman coin. The one produced bore the profile of Tiberius. This prompted his answer: Give Caesar his things and God what is his. But in Caiaphas the temple caste had an experienced collaborator with the Romans. His High Priesthood was the longest of the century between Herod the Great's accession and the destruction of Jerusalem. An opportunist's co-operation with Pontius Pilate had enabled him to form an accurate picture of the man on whose decision the immediate fate of Jesus would depend.

CHAPTER NINETEEN

Pontius Pilate

Only one character in the life of Jesus, outside the circle of his friends, his mother and his betrayer, achieves memorability, and he is from the west. Appropriately, for it is a specific quality of the west to give its characters contrasting qualities, Pilate can be classified neither with the good nor the bad. In this he is a true outsider to the Levant. The middle east sees men and women in the contrasts of a landscape where whites are glaring and shadows inky. This tendency endures. Medieval Arab rulers were considered to possess every virtue, like Saladin, or every weakness, like al-Hakim, the mad anti-Caliph who enforced a twenty-four hour curfew on women.[1] It would be wrong to attribute this black-and-white approach solely to one geographical area, for great rages can scorch deep shades in every climate: few westerners can yet see Heinrich Himmler in double focus – the murderous police chief sobbing with gratitude when Count Bernadotte presented him with a Swedish volume on Nordic runes, his favourite subject; and as late as 1980 a New Statesman publicist attacked Diana Mosley for describing Dr Goebbels as 'clever and witty', as if such qualities were inconceivable of an ally of Hitler.

Pilate had aroused similarly exclusive judgments. The Jews, in words quoted by Philo, found him 'inflexible, merciless, obstinate'. The Christian tendency has been to advance from the relatively balanced portrait given by the gospels through positive approval to *de facto* canonisation.[2]

Pilate must be approached in terms of his function. Italian-born and probably of freedman origin, he was one of hundreds of similar functionaries employed by the Caesars to run their empire; a class, in the

---

[1] 'As is so frequently the case with the "Lives" of the Christian saints, the "Lives" of the great Muslim mystics are told in such a manner as to obliterate the distinctive peculiarities both of character and of fate. They are individualized just enough to establish their typological genuineness and their position within the hierarchy of the type.' Gustave E. von Grünebaum: *Medieval Islam*, Chicago, 1948: p. 223.

[2] *The Gospel of Peter* makes Herod, not Pilate, pass the fatal sentence; a third-century Syrian work, *Didaskalia Apostolorum*, denies that Pilate consented to the deeds of the wicked Jews. Tertullian (*Apologeticus* XXI) thinks of him already as a Christian at heart. He and his wife Procla achieve halos in Coptic and Ethiopic art.

words of an authority, that might lapse by an easy declension into
torpor or corruption.[1] Pilate entered history when he took over the
Roman province of Syria (which included Judaea, Samaria and
Idumaea) in AD 26. His wife Procla, like the wives of many western
envoys to the east, seems to have been interested in the country where
he served but his own approach to local attitudes was high-handed and
contemptuous. The loss of a major section of the *Annals* of Tacitus unfortunately makes it impossible to quiz this key figure through one
sharp lens. We miss an acid summation of the events of Pilate's ten-
year prefecture: possibly including the most important.[2]

The same gap in the *Annals* robs us of a dramatic occurrence which
gives the background to Pilate's hesitations. Lucius Aelius Sejanus
was the procurator's patron. Sejanus had made himself the virtual
ruler of Rome, first by advising Tiberius to retire to Capri, then by
exploiting his links with the pretorian guard, which his father had
commanded. To inherit the purple from Tiberius he had four of the
emperor's relations poisoned, including his son Drusus. But his own
fate showed that in old age Tiberius remained the master plotter. A
missive of ruthless dissimulation was read to the Senate. Its opening
terms combined fulsome praise of Sejanus with hints of his promotion
to greater favour. The lulled favourite took in, too late, the letter's icy
turn. It denounced his reason and commanded his instant execution.

Such falls were common, though rarely contrived with such spiteful
finesse. They bred insecurity in delegated rulers.

Yet Pilate's class had the same inbred merits as the public school officials who administered the British empire. The ruthless Pilate had
been educated in a curriculum which taught how to lead a sentence to a
euphonious conclusion. Like other Roman schoolboys he was fam-
iliarised not only with rhetorical arguments for the simple life or the
claims of patriotism, but with a knowledge of such teachers as Plato,
Zeno and Epicurus. In the decoration of his palace, in the arrangement
of his dinners, he was no barbarian. The survival of the soul after
death, the nature of true courage, such dinner topics were discussed
after the suppression of a riot or the deduction of temple funds to
finance an aqueduct. In his reflective moments he was closer to the universalism of Alexandria than the narrowness of Rome. Probably the
thing he liked best in Jerusalem was its climate, brisker than that of
humid Caesarea. And unless we assume that Jesus was impressive to

---

[1] Syme: op.cit., p. 441: note 5.
[2] Ibid, p. 449. 'The missing books (VII to X) will have furnished ample compensation
(for comparative silence on the Levant earlier) – faction at Alexandria and the strife of
Greek against Jew. Also several episodes concerning Judaea: princes and the intract-
able people and the vicissitudes of the Roman procurators, not omitting Pontius
Pilatus. . . .'

Levantines only, it is not surprising if his words and actions, distorted or magnified by rumour, intrigued the prefect. His wife had certainly seen or heard him to the point where even her dreams were invaded.

To persuade an official as urbane as Pilate to put Jesus to death for purely religious reasons would be impossible. To the Roman expatriate, all eastern religions were superstitions, *curiosa* to be discussed rather as nineteen centuries later the author of *Studies in Brown Humanity* would discuss the customs of another empire over a Lagos dinner.[1] And once Pilate recognised the non-violent nature of the defendant's ideas, it was predictable that the colonial suspicion which attaches to the thug or dervish would evaporate. Such a prediction was correct. Pilate was to find the mouths shouting for death or the minds contriving it less to his taste than the hypnotic figure immobile before him.

The high priest's problem was therefore to persuade Pontius Pilate that the disturbances caused by Jesus were certain to increase and in doing so to involve political dangers. The problem of making a conviction on one ground acceptable on another is perennial, and soluble. It could be solved with Jesus. The charge on which the High Priest and his advisers had informally condemned him was that of being a false prophet and a practitioner of magic. But in order to secure the connivance of a state which regarded the Torah with indifference, Jesus had to be presented as a threat to Roman rule – and, in particular, to Pilate's reputation.

In theory, the charge of magic involved penalties under Roman as well as Jewish law. But like the edicts which were issued regularly but vainly to curb extravagance in dress, edicts against occult practice were hard to enforce. It was not easy to distinguish between white magic and black, between fortune-telling and the use of lethal spells. On this score the evidence of Judas could convince the clergy, not the prefect. Pilate would classify Judas as a police informer with a lively imagination and a grudge against a former friend.

[1] Sir Hugh Clifford: *Further India*, London, 1904.

CHAPTER TWENTY

The Last Symposium

Those who study even an ordinary life tend to read back into it design rather than accident. The life of Jesus is extraordinary by any standards. One extraordinary aspect is our dependence for our knowledge of it on the later writings of his followers and our necessity to push behind these writings to the facts that they often conceal. These followers lived in a Hellenistic climate which assumed that gods could intermarry with mortals or appear to them in mortal disguise. That Jesus had been an incarnate god became a common belief, though the precise way in which divinity coalesced with humanity was to perplex theologians for several centuries. The gospel-writers, or those who edited their texts for publication, would have found it incredible that things could happen to a god without his planning or foreknowledge. Thus our four main sources unite in giving his last days the momentum of a drama in which protagonist and dramatist are one. Jesus weeps over the holy but murderous city since, possessing divine foreknowledge, he foresees its doom, on the 9th of Ab, some forty summers later. He enters Jerusalem knowing that he is about to die. The divine man eats with his friends fully conscious that on this planet he will not drink wine again. In an enacted metaphor of his emphasis on love, he washes his friends' feet, dressed in a towel like the humblest servant. John holds up his particular momentum by inserting a farewell discourse. He probably composed this much later at Ephesus, weaving it together from sentences heard at various times in his friendship with Jesus; unintentionally he gives it a garrulity more fitted to an old man than the terse young foreigner.

At this distance of time, squinting through the palings of our four accounts, we can only surmise how much he knew or suspected. A miscalculation of the risks may have lured him into Jerusalem. He may have credited his enemies with prudence – even compassion – that they did not possess. His mind may have been preoccupied with an experiment planned for later that evening: a variant on the mystery of Bethany. Or his last visit to Jerusalem may have been routine. He may have divided his waking hours between public speech, private visits to men and women who accepted his teaching, and evenings devoted to his friends and new recruits. Most men everywhere assume that things will go on as they are now forever. Yet to all men comes the last visit to the clothes shop, the last convivial evening, the last drink of water. If Jesus was not supernaturally aware that the storm was about to burst, he had lived for some time with the sound of thunder.

While the accounts of his last meal conflict with one another, and while all have been impressed with a particular symbolism,[1] all four agree that Jesus ate with his disciples for the last time on a Thursday evening. Other details, particularly in John, give the meal convincing affinities with the supper parties held in Hellenistic Alexandria and Ephesus but also among the Romanised classes in Palestine itself. But this symposium is under the menace of treachery. It is not lightened by banter or speculation. Jesus himself drains the atmosphere of conviviality when he predicts that one of those present is planning to betray him. Peter signals to the favourite disciple, apparently reclining on Jesus's bosom, to discover which of them was meant.

Jesus answers.

'It is the one to whom I give this piece of food which I am about to dip in the dish.'[2]

The scene is still familiar to those who, dining with Arabs or Arabised Jews, dip into a large central dish which might be couscous in Morocco or *kouzi ala timan* – lamb with rice – in Iraq. Fingers are used, not knives and forks. But when the food is semi-liquid, a fragment of flat bread is bent to form a convenient shovel.

For all its realism the incident could well be fiction. It detracts from the surprise which, shortly afterwards, in another place, Jesus shows when approached by Judas. It fits too conveniently into a triad of predicted betrayals. For after Judas it is the turn of the disciples to be warned of their weakness.

'Listen! The time will come, in truth it has come already, when you will be scattered, each going his own way and leaving me deserted.'[3]

And when after the meal Peter protests that he at least will never abandon Jesus, he is snubbed by the assertion that before cockcrow he will have disowned him thrice.

Yet, true or false, the incident testifies to the impression Jesus made on those who knew him. He was the kind of man who could construe the future from the hearts of those who would make it.

The sad note of treachery, sounded by the betrayers or their friends, must be linked, however, with two facts, not one. The flight of the dis-

[1] For an examination of the gospel-writers' assumption that Jesus died in early spring, and that his death was the symbolic equivalent of the slaughter of the Passover lamb, see Appendix B.
[2] John 13, 26: DS.
[3] John 16, 32: JB/DS.

ciples is the dispiriting but normal reaction of an unarmed band to the arrest of its leader. A beardless youth and a pack of women will escort Jesus to his execution. But something abnormal, something which will change history, is also to happen. The disciples will become convinced, from the greatest to the last, that in abandoning Jesus they have abandoned, not the victim, but the victor. The active traitor, in committing suicide, will show himself more swiftly perspicacious than the others.

After supper, Jesus and his disciples, but without Judas who has pleaded an excuse to leave, eat bread and drink wine in a ceremony whose significance Jesus had explained long ago in Capernaum – at the expense of outraging many Galileans. They then cross the Kedron valley, dry in summer, to a private domain owned by friends and used (before umbrella pines replaced the olives which gave this district its name) for the production of oil. Jesus has what seems a sudden foreboding; it could be the need to be alone or with a new disciple. He tells Peter and two others to await some way off but to keep alert. In fact, after the food and drink, after the strain of recent days, they fall asleep. Their lack of apprehension suggests it was a common experience for their leader to withdraw alone, or in the company of some new recruit. Mark was later to insert, in the somnolence of Peter and the others, a long prayer in which Jesus asks God to avert his doom. Who heard this prayer, and recalled it, is not recorded. But a concrete detail from the information Mark received suggests why Jesus chose this solitary place for nocturnal meetings. At the climax of the evening, when Judas indeed approaches and the disciples scatter, the temple police catch hold of a young man dressed in nothing but a length of linen over his naked body. 'But he left the shroud in their hands and ran off naked.'[1]

But for this clue we might have pictured the garden as simply the place where Jesus escaped the nocturnal city's congested lanes. Such escape is a middle east tradition. In modern Damascus taverns throng the gorge of the Barada just as classical Alexandria had resorts by the Nile's Canopic outlet. But Gethsemane was no tavern or place of common resort. Behind its walls, among its trees, Jesus was accustomed to come for a purpose.

What was it?

Here for the last time we see him as a free individual, the finder of the dragon-surrounded pearl, the foreigner who brings truths of great price. We dare not shirk the attempt to surmise what he felt his purpose to be. He certainly did not see himself as the political liberator of one ethnic group. We may confidently ascribe the few passages which put this view to the theology of Matthew. An ethical man, he did not claim to be important as the purveyor of a new ethical system. And

[1] Mark 14, 52: JB/DS.

although he was a healer, an exorcist, a man who could work prodigies, others have done such things without making his claims. At baptism, the key moment in his life, a power had descended on him from the realm of the sun. He was, he then knew, the envoy of this power. And linked to this role was the conviction that he was an envoy to future envoys with whom, through the generations, he would remain connected. If he was to return to the god which he characteristically distinguished from *to archon tou kosmou toutou*, 'the ruler of this cosmos', to become one with this true god, then the process of self-deification, the taking on of the powers he had shown, was to be the quality of those he left behind.[1] Like all creatures under the sun, Jesus, on the road to identification with the Sun behind the sun, was subject to the laws of growth. The cycle of egg, caterpillar, chrysalis, moth, is only one spectacular instance of this law. Every plant, animal, mind, grows by stages.

If we accept the concept of a Jesus who experiments, we can see in part why such contradictory views of him have been entertained, each concentrating on one phase at the expense of the whole. But apart from the cures, the exorcisms, the temporary control of weather and natural forces, his deepest experiments were to do with acted symbol. Professor Morton Smith, the rediscoverer of the Marcan Lazarus, hints towards a spiritual baptism which may not have excluded erotic connotations. Some of the gnostic material now accessible to us through the publication of the Coptic library long buried at Nag Hammadi supports such a view. But the evidence of Bethany indicates that Jesus practised a species of mystery akin to what Lucius Apuleius experienced in the cult of Isis. Apuleius was forbidden to disclose the pagan rituals whose culmination nevertheless brought him such rapture that he regarded the occasion as a new beginning, a new birthday. Yet he says this much to his readers:

> I approached the very gates of death and set foot on Proserpine's threshold, yet was permitted to return, rapt through all the elements. At midnight I saw the sun shining as if it were noon; I entered the presence of the gods of the under-world and the gods of the upper-world, stood near and worshipped them.[2]

Because Jesus was killed – or if we prefer another view, recalled to the kingdom of the east – before he could record, or get others to record, the form these mysteries took, we can, with one exception, only speculate. The exception is the ceremony of eating bread and drinking wine which goes under the title of the eucharist.

[1] John 14, 12. 'The man that believes in me, the works that I do, and greater works than I do, shall he accomplish.'
[2] Apuleius: *The Golden Ass*; tr. Robert Graves, London, 1950.

Our evidence for this is older than for Jesus's trial or crucifixion. Less than thirty years after the last supper Paul was adverting to it in a letter:

> For this is what I have received from the Lord, and in turn passed on to you: that on the same night that he was betrayed the Lord Jesus took some bread and thanked God for it and broke it, and he said, 'This is my body, which is broken for you: do this as a memorial of me.' In the same way he took the cup after supper, and said, 'This cup is the new covenant in my blood. Whenever you drink it, do this as a memorial for me.'[1]

Since Paul quotes the Lord as his informant, we cannot be sure how much derives from human witness and how much has been filtered through his often topsy-turvy amalgam of Jewish and Hellenic ideas. The reference to a 'new covenant' almost certainly springs from theories of his own. But what Jesus did is clear enough. He took bread and wine, elements of everyday sociability which yet mark the heights of Osirian symbolism and transformed them, not into a sacrifice, but a bond between two states of being. Bread stales and wine goes sour. They are the products of time. But now they signify the unlocalised, the timeless. Here I find it impossible not to quote a modern source – the Japanese novelist Shusaku Endo.[2] 'It is by instituting the sacrament of the Eucharist' – Richard A. Schuchert, a Jesuit, is the translator – 'that Jesus demonstrates his overwhelming desire to remain beyond his death and forever the inseparable companion of every human being.'

Did Jesus practise another rite in the secluded garden? If so, what was it? We are left with speculation. The shroud-like cloth let slip by the youth recalls the simulated death of Lazarus. For night, with a darkened Jerusalem lit by infrequent blurs on the western skyline, Jesus had possibly devised a physical action which symbolised the hour and its hidden content. To the Egyptians who honoured Rê, to the coastal cities whose chief city honoured him as Hêlios, the sun was not dead in the hours of darkness.[3] He was traversing the other side of nature. The immortalising gnosis hidden behind the garments and customs of daily life resembles the hidden sun of the midnight garden. This gnosis is the pearl of great price. For only when a man knows who he is, where he comes from and where he is going, can his flame burn

[1] 1 Corinthians 11, 23–26: JB.
[2] Shusako Endo: *A Life of Jesus*, Tokyo, 1978.
[3] Marcus Diaconus, in his life of Porphyry, Bishop of Gaza, reports that Hêlios was the prime god in eight public temples along the Palestinian coast, having precedence over Aphrodite, Apollo, Persephone, Hecate, Tychê, etc. Hêlios also appears on the coins of Ascalon.

steady and bright to transcend the transient. The gnosis plays the role of the unmoving fulcrum on which even the world's weight can theoretically be lifted.

But torches and the flash of light on steel awake the disciples. Judas appears among the trees. In fulfilment of the agreement he made with the priests he has led the armed men to the secret garden. He will use a kiss, the common salutation among middle eastern males, to identify a man the guards know only by report and to effect an arrest with the minimum of fuss. He uses the word rabbi – the equivalent of *didaskalos* in Greece or *guru* in India – to compound his treachery. For the tragedy of Jesus has passed the point of possible return. It is no longer a question of doubting a mission. It is a question of trapping the man he once loved to an end he can envisage.

Jesus answers.

'Comrade, what are you here for?'

Before Judas answers, the solders seize their quarry. One of his followers draws a sword. A temple guard is wounded. The flash of violence provokes Jesus to his solitary protest.

'You arrest me as if I were a terrorist. And yet I was accessible to you daily, preaching in your temple.'

His disciples have vanished and his arms are bound. His passion has started.

CHAPTER TWENTY-ONE

Ah, Truth, What Is That?

Jesus's trial and conviction belong to secular as well as religious history. Yet for our knowledge of what happened we are still confined to four accounts where details conflict and whose theological presuppositions distort the narrative. There is a total lack of neutral or hostile material to serve as a check. The relevant books of Tacitus (which may have said something) are lost; the Talmudic references to Jesus are late and obscure.

One thing seems plain: the priests needed to involve three separate parties in the drama they planned. The Pharisees – earnest, independent-minded scholars, sometimes hair-splitting, often lenient – devoted their lives to the interpretation and protection of the law, oral as well as written. They would have to be persuaded that in punishing Jesus they would be destroying a heretical apostate. On a very different level, a noisy crowd would be needed, to clamour at the right moment for the death of a deviant. And most problematic, Pontius Pilate, representative of the Roman state, must be convinced that Jesus threatened imperial stability, not merely some quirk of the Mosaic law.

The Pharisees, far more numerous in Judaea than Galilee, had heard enough of Jesus on his appearances in Jerusalem to be predisposed against him. Though his ethical teaching hardly differed from theirs, they had been shocked by rumours of the incident at Bethany. There was good reason to believe that Jesus had entered a tomb; standing within defiling distance of a corpse, he had revived it by necromancy or fraud. Although the evidence for this came from a single witness (not the two required by law) Judas was as convincing on Bethany as on other aspects of Jesus's mission.

A noisy mob was easy to muster. Indignation could easily be aroused by what he had said about the temple: it was, as people were particularly mindful in August, a vulnerable institution. His non-violence exasperated those who saw terrorists under detention as national heroes. Money could plug emotional gaps.

This left Pilate.

Outwardly a Jewish High Priest and a Roman prefect had little in common. To Caiaphas, Pontius Pilate was a gentile oppressor guilty of high-handed and ruthless acts. To Pilate, Caiaphas was the priest of a superstition which he regarded with distaste. But such obstacles were trivial to an alliance of interest. Colonial administrators have always made it their business to induce individual natives, or better still, a native class, to identify their cause with that of the alien ruler. Such individuals or classes have echoed Caiaphas's maxim: 'it is better for one man to die for the people, than for the whole nation to be destroyed.'[1] Some Roman administrators were more principled than Pilate. Pliny the Younger, for example, was to compose letters which reveal a tolerant, observant man. Yet under instruction from his second-century emperor, Pliny would send persistent Christians to the swordsman without anguish. Pilate's education, a century earlier, spoke in contrasted tongues. Hellenic humanism was one voice; Roman realism was the other and stronger.

Caiaphas had convinced Pilate, probably earlier in the week, at the latest on the eve of the last supper, that Jesus was likely to cause a disturbance in the holy city. The priest's prescience cannot be faulted. He stood closer to history than the New Testament authors; these wrote when Jews had become objects of maximum suspicion; the gospel-writers played down the anti-Roman feeling common in the Palestine that was to explode into the revolt of AD 66. Yet hardly a month in the decade Pilate and Caiaphas worked together – from four years before the crucifixion to six years after it – was unshadowed by hints of popular unrest. Acts of military oppression, collective punishments, crucifixions, were palliatives only.

John preserves evidence which confirms this co-operation between priest and prefect. Judas, John tells us in his account of the betrayal, was familiar with the garden where Jesus spent his evenings. 'He brought the cohort to this place together with a detachment of guards sent by the chief priests and the Pharisees, all with lanterns and torches and weapons.'[2] Jesus was not to appear before Pilate on the Friday morning as some unknown traffic violator before a magistrate. He was a man with a dossier to whose arrest and interrogation Pilate had assented.

The armed hirelings of what was for once a diarchy converged on the Mount of Olives. The mixed force had specific advantages. For a posse of temple guards alone to have arrested Jesus outside the walls could have seemed an invasion of Roman rights; the presence of troops from the Roman garrison expressed the interest of Rome; from the Mount they could escort Jesus to his interrogation by a representative of his own *ethnos*, or people. Thus far, no further. The sight of Roman sol-

[1] John 11, 50: JB.
[2] John 18, 2–4: JB.

diers intruding on a priestly palace would not be helpful. The atmosphere of diarchical collusion would be soured if Annas, a former High Priest, accepted a Jewish prisoner from uncircumcised pork-eaters marching under idols.

His hands bound, Jesus was hurried back across the Kedron wadi to the dark metropolis. At the moment of his capture Jesus had seen the night as symbolising the temporary power of evil.[1] It protected the scattered disciples who had fled among the trees. Panic-stricken, they sensed that their leader, not they, was the hunters' quarry. The naked youth, his initiation interrupted, escaped privately to ponder whether he had been told fantasies, or truths. Peter and an unnamed disciple discreetly followed the tramping soldiers.

Annas had been waiting in his lamp-lit palace. He started his interrogation as the young disciple, with some difficulty and at the cost of Peter's dissimulation, got them both into the palace.

Annas was old, shrewd and still influential thanks to his daughter's marriage to Caiaphas. None of the witnesses to Annas's inquisition was a supporter of Jesus. Only a garbled version of the old man's questions leaked from the sombre circle. John reports two questions: who constituted Jesus's disciples? What doctrines did he teach?[2] These are the questions, if we substitute cell and ideology for disciples and doctrines, put to middle east dissidents today, with the first electric shocks. The order in which they are put shows authority's abiding concerns. Is the organisation large enough to be a danger? (The ease with which Jesus had been taken was a good sign: only one of his followers had resisted.) The doctrinal charge (as Mark preserves it[3]) was his claimed ability to destroy the temple and rebuild it. This charge indeed smacked of fantasy. Yet it showed a bias against the priestly class and opened a useful approach to Pilate. The building of temples, in Israel no less than Egypt, was an attribute of kingship.

'I have always spoken in public, in synagogues and in the temple,' John quotes Jesus as replying. 'I have said nothing in secret. Ask those who heard me what I taught.'[4]

One of the guards slaps Jesus for impertinence. John's report, if correct, would show Jesus as disingenuous; more probably, it is invented. According to the synoptics, Jesus had visited Jerusalem only once; according to John he had spoken in one synagogue.[5] The evidence for these figures is shaky, but certainly Jesus liked preaching in the open air: once, for instance, from a boat moored near the shore; Matthew

[1] Luke 22, 53.
[2] John 19, 19.
[3] Mark 14, 58.
[4] John 18, 21–22: DS.
[5] John 6, 59.

has him delivering a sermon on a hillock, Luke on a level plain. A nocturnal discussion with Nicodemus early in his mission, his tête-à-tête with the woman by the Samarian well, are two instances of private if not secret teaching.

Annas finally sends Jesus to Caiaphas, probably to arrange an equivalent of an American Grand Jury, with the Sanhedrin as jurymen. Caiaphas may have had quarters elsewhere in the sprawling building, or he may have had a palace of his own. We do not know.

John omits the nocturnal trial by the Sanhedrin described by Mark and Matthew. From what we know of Sanhedrin procedure, a formal trial by night was hardly likely. Most, if not all, of its seventy members had already concluded that he was a false prophet who could seduce the simple-minded, a magician: accusations close in spirit to those brought against Socrates by his Athenian enemies. Luke reports a trial at daybreak.[1]

The official Roman day began at sunrise, but in any case, Pilate would have risen early. Sharing a room with Procla, he had had an insomniac night; but he was also interested to see the dissident he had discussed with Caiaphas.

Hearing the clamour outside the Pretorium, Pilate paces into the open to meet the Jews. He knows this strange people's abhorrence of contacts with other nations, their particular dislike of a headquarters where representations of Julius Caesar, Augustus, Roman eagles, clutter the entrance.

'What is the charge against the accused?'

'If he were not a malefactor, would we have brought him?'

Pilate assumes, for the record, that he hears the charge for the first time and that it involves a religious law preoccupied by such bans as the consumption of meat and milk on the same occasion.

'We are not empowered to carry out death sentences.'

The word death makes the stakes visible. There follows the most dramatic dialogue in the New Testament. The timeless bisects the linear. The honours of this world collide with the undefined glories of another. The stranger from the kingdom of the east, the god of the Europe that is to be, opposes the serpent, the pearl's coiling warder. Jesus is to conquer much in Pilate himself but in a matter of years the serpent will constrict what Jesus stands for; what in his stand can be distorted, will be.

Who hears and reports this dialogue between the *archon* of matter and the *archon* of spirit? Guards in breastplates and greaves stand with their swords drawn. They half understand Pilate's Greek. At some point Procla's woman interrupts with a plea from her mistress, troubled all night by dreams of Jesus. On a visit to the bazaar, she had

[1] Luke 22, 66.

seen him from her litter. Procla herself, haggard, her long maquillage half started, may have stood within earshot. Or the unnamed Judaean disciple may have had access here as well as to the palace of Annas. He was on terms of friendship with the sacerdotal dynasty. Hellenised young men were not bothered by the proximity of porphyry sculptures.

Luke (more of a historian than his confrères) tells us that the Jews brought three charges against Jesus: revolutionary agitation; incitement to the non-payment of tribute; claiming to be the messiah, a king.[1] Since Luke knows that the first two charges are false, this could be proof, if we need more, that the claim implicit in the third charge was not made by Jesus.

Yet it is the third charge that Pilate takes seriously.

'Are you the king of the Jews?'

He phrases the question in the manner of the psychiatrist who asks if the patient is really the Duke of Edinburgh? But the threats to the temple are attested. They could prove that Jesus was dangerous as well as deranged.

'Is this your own question? Or have you been put up to it by others?'

Jesus shows nothing of the cringing suppliant. So far he has only been betrayed, bound and slapped.

'You don't suppose I am a Jew? It's your own authorities who have delivered you to me. Be frank: what is your offence?'

'My followers did not use force to prevent the Jews taking me. That proves my kingdom is not of this earth.'

'Yet you are some kind of king?'

'Your metaphor. I am a king in this sense: I came into the world, I was born, for one purpose only, to reveal the truth; and those who respond to truth respond to what I say.'

'Ah, truth.' The world-weary voice is a sound of Europe: it echoes from Greek sophists to Maugham and Malraux. 'What on earth is that?'

The verbal game cannot continue. The prisoner, for all the depth in his eyes, is a *naïf*; for all his courage, simple. The Roman leaves him for the hot sun.

'I find no legal case against him.'

'But you plan,' the jeer-leaders retort, 'to execute three guerillas. On much less evidence. In the case of Barabbas, invented evidence.'[2]

The crowd in unison: 'Release Barabbas!'

Nothing frightens an imperialist so much as a riot. The shouts, the

[1] Luke 22, 2.

[2] That Barabbas was a Jewish nationalist held on unconvincing evidence seems less like a fairy-tale than the custom, claimed only in the gospels, of the annual release of a political prisoner.

gestures, put Pilate's hankering for Jesus in perspective. But it exists still. He hands him over to his soldiers' horseplay. The mob may fall silent when they see the weals of a Roman scourging, the furrows ploughed by bored young athletes.

But the priests have chosen their crowd.

Pilate leads Jesus into the open, a thorn diadem crushed on his head, a cheap red robe hanging wet on his exhausted body. They have done much, the young men, and quickly.

'Here's the man,' says Pilate, 'you're making this fuss about.'

The prefect is not surprised, he has seen gladiators howled to death, as they keep up the chorus: 'Crucify him! Crucify him!'

But he is disgusted.

'Crucify him yourselves.' He is a gentleman, of the equestrian, not the patrician, order; similar to the public schoolboys who ran the British empire on Dr Arnold's model: a blend of the classics, biblical pieties, practicality. Modest to their betters, not to others.

'I can still find no case against him.'

'But under our law, someone who claims to be God's son deserves execution.'

Pilate is at the wrong point in history to smile at this assertion. Two generations before Julius Caesar, dry, rational, witty, had been declared a god at his funeral. His great-nephew, whom Pilate remembers, was honoured in a divine diptych with Rome even in his lifetime. The shadow of such deifications lengthens before him. Seneca will mock the next emperor but one, a stuttering pedant: *The Pumpkinification of Claudius*. In the lifetime of the youngest men present Domitian will sign his correspondence, *Divus et Dominus*. The absurd notion is not new. Platonists believe their philosopher was begotten platonically. Olympias, the mother of Alexander, was impregnated by an Olympian, not by King Philip. The world is as full of prodigies as dangers. If there are divine men, what would one look like?

Pilate stumbles back into the marbled shadows. He has flicker vision. A painless migraine. One moment he sees the imperial busts, then Jesus, incandescent.

'Where,' Pilate whispers, 'do you come from?'

Not, from what village or district. We have your dossier. What terrain, further than Alexandria, further than the Pillars of Hercules: what cold flat shore from which the earth floats like a silver platter? His arms are suddenly chilled under the toga. He has to sit down. But Jesus is silent and Pilate needs a chair.

'You refuse to answer? Yet I can command your crucifixion.'

As the howls continue, Pilate beckons. Jesus follows. The prefect slumps majestically in a splendid chair, head bowed. A voice shrieks across the sun-dazzled pavement.

'If you befriend this man, you are no friend to Caesar.'

Common sense wins. It will be cheaper to release Barabbas. In his calm moments Pilate acknowledges, like most of his contemporaries, that the torturer gets the answers he wants, not true information. Barabbas was tortured; his evidence was worthless. Instead of Barabbas this man can hang between the others. The terror of ideas is perhaps worse than the terror of daggers. But Pilate will annoy the Levantines, if only to make up for the night he's in for with Procla.

In his own hand he writes: *Jesus Rex Judaeorum*. Under it: *Iesous Basileus Ton Ioudaion*.

His secretary bows. The large letters tell him that Pilate has a headache. 'Shall I complete it in the local language?'

His letters slither from right to left.

The action is watched and understood by the Jews.

'Change it!' shouts a furious voice. 'Write *The Self-Proclaimed*.'

'Enough,' says Pilate. 'What I have written, I have written.'

He could have the whole pack of them tortured, if he wished to.

The air smells fresher as the mob departs, a flame at its centre.

CHAPTER TWENTY-TWO

Crucifixion

The crucifixion of dissidents was an everyday chore to the detachment of soldiers detailed to deal with Jesus. If a Judaean newspaper had existed, a crucifixion would have commanded less space in its pages than the dust-storm which was to make the execution barely visible.

In Jesus's boyhood two thousand Jews had been crucified in Palestine when Varus, the legate imported from Syria, had used this frightening method to crush a revolt (the first of many). As a mode of judicial killing, crucifixion was protracted, painful and messy. Its combination of pain and delay distinguished it from stoning, decapitation or burning with firewood. Healthy subjects could last for several days in moderate weather. A century earlier gentlemen on horseback, ladies in litters, had held their noses as they passed the recaptured followers of Spartacus, strung as on telegraph poles along Italy's chief highway. As physical pain subdued even the strongest, loss of sphincter control produced physical ordure which broke the victims' spirits and repelled their admirers.

Even in ordinary cities, it was usual for executions to be conducted outside the inhabited areas and often, like burials, along a roadside. In the case of a city as special as Jerusalem public opinion insisted that human blood should be spilt on the outskirts. As the purpose of execution was in part to deter, a site by a main road had obvious advantages.

The place chosen for Jesus's death was on the northern side of the holy city. It took its name, Golgotha, a cranium, either from the debris of unfortunates or, more likely, from the proximity of a rocky outcrop whose apertures recalled a skull's sockets.[1]

The small procession made its way towards this place of ill name through narrow streets. Since in Roman eyes Jesus was a political

---

[1] The location of Golgotha can no longer be confidently asserted. The area identified by the Empress Irene with Calvary and the holy sepulchre has a dubious claim, being so close to the temple and what must have been an inhabited area. The small cliff overlooking the bus-station and so-called Garden Tomb has the right appearance. The early fifth-century Acts of Pilate has the prefect sentencing Jesus to be 'hanged upon the cross in the garden in which you were arrested'. This would put Golgotha on the slopes of the Mount of Olives.

criminal, the title proclaiming him King of the Jews played the role of the placards which other societies affix to those due to be shot or hanged. His male disciples, those who could have given some show to his satiric title, were in hiding, with one exception. But a group of women, enjoying a middle eastern immunity, followed with the dreary ululations reserved for mourning. They roused in turn the same scurrilous malice, the curses and insults as accompanied later victims to the bonfire or guillotine. The one male supporter was the well-connected youth who had obtained admission for Peter to the High Priest's palace, where the senior disciple had then fulfilled the prediction of a triple denial. According to John, three at least of the women persisted to the place of execution. It makes sense that his mother was the chief among them. There was little in her stepchildren's Galilee household to tempt her to stay there. Joseph's oldest and most pious son, James, will have found her a painful reminder of a family scandal. Joset will have carped at the cost of her upkeep while his wife will have fretted at her airs and graces. Her closest ally was probably a second Mary, the wife of Joseph's younger brother, Clopas, or Cleopatros. Like Mary of Joseph, Mary of Clopas had known the world outside this neurotic ghetto and doubtless regretted it. The third and last Mary – to be sometimes named, like Jesus's mother, as Miriam[1] – was a former whore. It has been fashionable to portray Mary of Magdala as fragilely beautiful. It is as reasonable to picture her as prematurely aged, her skin dry from farded evenings in which eyes flickered between hope of gain and psychic tension. Like many prostitutes, Mary had doubtless ceased to find males attractive. What drew her to Jesus was his remoteness from the lures of the flesh, the casements he opened on a world where she could be taken seriously as a being, not as a body devalued month by month as her labours took their toll.

The weather has thickened. Dawn brightness has yielded to that opaque glare which, when the wind veers from across the Jordan, promises the migration of a million sandy particles to inflame the small vessels of throat and ear and tire the eyes: weather to induce thirst among those lolling on shady cushions but agony among those cut off, till they faint, from the petty reliefs which make life supportable. Jesus, unused to rough handling, has been the sport of a brutal young regiment. But, gashed from his scourging, he is forced to shoulder the bar which forms the horizontal section of his cross. The word cross is a misnomer if one imagines the traditional symbol in churches, let alone the heraldic devices linked with Lorraine or Malta. The penal cross can be compared to a gigantic Greek *tau*, or sanserif T. It is also an echo of one of the hieroglyphs used by the Egyptians for Set, the strange half-brother of Osiris whom an authority describes as 'an anti-social

[1]   Matthew 28, 1; John 20, 16 & 18.

god, cut off from the community of gods':⊥¹.

The bar's weight causes Jesus to stumble. The soldiers, eager to be done, conscript a bystander to handle it for him. The bustling street gives way to a sallow place of scorched vegetation. A young man gallops north to Nablus on the road below; slower travellers brood on money, or the girl at the evening's inn.

On a level stretch of rock three sockets are empty for the uprights. Two other victims are being made ready. They are stripped of their bloody rags and their hands and feet attached with ropes to the assembled gibbet, stretched flat on the ground. The pull of the arms will hurt; but the phallic protuberance from the permanent upright will take some of their weight, prolonging and insulting their pains. Jesus too is stripped. He wears nothing but the crown whose crisp thorns parody the rays of the diadem worn by Hêlios in his statues. He is lifted to a place of mock honour between the others. All his weight pulls on his arms. Now, to those experienced in such things, begins a tedious process. The experienced centurion and his soldiers play games with bone dice. Minor perquisites compensate their boredom: baksheesh from the victims' relations if they give an opiate or quick *coup de grâce*; then the clothes. The spectators stand back. They are torn between a wish for the victim to stave off death and a longing for his death to release them to their normal routine. The victim feels much the same, though in the case of the violent, the hope of vengeance hardly assuages the knowledge of defeat.

Jesus has one advantage. He is but a week from a triumph over simulated death. He is now to essay the next stage, but in earnest. John, decades later, was to remember a mood of tentative triumph. But John would remember it when all was accomplished and pain forgotten. Now Jesus suffers. In the increasing heat, he thirsts. Yet, like the masochist in sadistic games, he is in control. John records an instance. The man on the cross finds strength to bind Mary to his disciple. Henceforth they are mother and son, son and mother. It is no routine commendation. Mary has at times caused him irritation, fussing over a coin lost from her necklace, accepting too intensely customs of hospitality, fretting at his association with a well-known harlot, even doubting his mission. But his love for her shows in his resolve to detach her from the family which has scorned his message but whose greed may yet try to exploit what will survive – and he has no false modesty – of his reputation. Jesus is thus in control into his final moments. Joseph's family would normally have taken her in when Jesus was dead but, still living, he snaps the traditional bond in favour of his disciple. Mary will play no part in the squabbles and successes of his Jerusalem adherents, soon

¹ H. Te Velde: *Seth, God of Confusion; A Study of his Role in Egyptian Mythology and Religion*, Leiden, 1967: p. 30.

to be ruled by Joseph's children.

By noon, the sultry heat has turned to dust storm. The watchers, including the soldiers, appear as shadows. The dispersal of his disciples is echoed by the desertion of the sun. It glows like a fickle moon behind the blackness. In response Jesus utters an enigmatic cry, usually taken to denote at least temporary despair. This may be due to a misunderstanding of what Jesus really said. The two gospel-writers who record it[1] take the cry to be the opening words of the Twenty-Second Psalm: My God, my God, why have you forsaken me? They transliterate the four Aramaic words in Greek letters. Both agree on the last two: *Lema sabachthani?* But their different transliterations of the first two words – *elôi elôi* in Mark, *êli êli* in Matthew – are curiously balanced by their agreement that bystanders understood Jesus to have called, not on God, but on Elias, or Elijah. One early gospel manuscript[2] has yet another interpretation which one major New Testament textual critic has accepted. This manuscript has the bystanders taking Jesus to be calling on Hêlios, not Elias. The vocative of Hêlios – or Êlios in the common pronunciation – is Êlie. In that case what Jesus cried has been re-interpreted by Christian tradition. If Jesus, at the climax of his life, was showing either an ironic ability to react, to the last, to the world of nature, or affinities to the cosmic view of the Hellenistic Levant, he would have been using, as was not uncommon, Greek and Aramaic in one sentence to cry:

O Sun! O Sun! Why have you forsaken me?[3]

Worn by every form of exhaustion, he let his head slump forward. The rays on his tawdry crown were all that was left to lighten the scene and the scene was dark.

When the soldiers, knowing the Jewish impatience to have the bodies away before the onset of the Sabbath, were to crack the bones of the other two victims, they stopped at him. He was dead already.

---

[1] Mark 15, 34 and Matthew 27, 46.
[2] The fourth or fifth-century Old Latin ms. *k*.
[3] For a longer discussion of the cry from the cross see Appendix C.

EPILOGUE

Burial And Reappearance

If Jesus had simply been executed for unpopular – or too popular – beliefs, specialists in the period might still know his name: they know, after all, of minor rebels against Roman authority or of actors once applauded by Roman crowds. But his impression on western civilisation would have been nil. Unlike Spartacus, he commanded no armed force; unlike Socrates, he left no distinctive philosophy and no disciple with the literary talents of Plato to develop his ideas. We have noted the contradictory ways in which the figure on the cross may be interpreted: as a messianic Hamlet abandoned by the power on which he had relied, or as a gnostic revealer buoyed through pain by awareness of a mission fulfilled. Yet there are no disputes about the mettle of his disciples. By the end they had dwindled to a handful of frightened men and mourning women. It could have been predicted, that last Friday evening, that they would blend into the mass, then take their recollections to silent graves.

Yet this was not to be the case. For what happened next, or seemed to happen, charged these fickle supporters with the confidence to alter history. Leaving Galilee for the city which had rejected Jesus, they were to inaugurate a religion which, in less than three centuries, would take over the Roman empire. His provincial kinsmen had assumed charge neither of his mother nor his dead body. Embarrassed by him when alive, they were yet to fill important posts in what may be called (with some hesitation) the Jerusalem church, and to suffer for so doing. The term bishop, like church, strikes a somewhat anachronistic note in the first century, but the nineteenth-century scholar Ernest Renan listed male connections of Jesus as Jerusalem's first four bishops. The first was James, Joseph's son; the second, Simeon, the son of Joseph's brother Clopas; the third, Judah, a grandson of Clopas; and the fourth, a great-grandson, Simeon II, martyred under Trajan. Two great-grandsons of Joseph (through another son, Jude) presided over churches elsewhere. They had the dangerous honour of being presented to the emperor Domitian.

The mystery which sets Jesus apart from other victims of judicial execution surrounds his burial, by no means the simple event which religious paintings might suggest.

Jesus had died around three on a Friday afternoon. John goes out of
his way to insert details that prove he was genuinely dead.[1]

The sequel was first described by Paul, in his first recorded address,
less than twenty years after the crucifixion. On a pioneer trip to what is
now central Turkey and was then southern Galatia, Paul was asked by
the presidents of the synagogue (who had no idea what to expect) to
address the congregation in Pisidian Antioch, a town close to the
modern Yalvac. The speech, which aroused gentile enthusiasm and
Jewish indignation, was carefully preserved and inserted in the Acts of
the Apostles.[2] The passage relating to Jesus's burial reads as follows:

> The people of Jerusalem and their rulers fulfilled, without realising
> it, the prophecies read out each sabbath. Though they found
> nothing to justify his death, they condemned him and asked Pilate to
> have him put to death. When they had accomplished all the scrip-
> tural predictions relating to him, they took him down from the tree
> and buried him in a tomb.[3]

The last statement strikingly differs from what was to become the
received opinion. Those who had prompted the crucifixion, Paul
claims, arranged the burial. When, a generation later, the gospel-
writers began arranging their own narratives of what had happened,
they were all to claim that a prominent Sanhedrin member had
arranged honorific sepulture for Jesus. This conflicts, it must be said,
with Mark's own statement that the whole Sanhedrin had condemned
Jesus and voted for his death.[4] But the enlistment of Joseph of Arimathea and Nicodemus, both Sanhedrin members, as supporters typifies
the myth-making found in underground movements.[5] Minds forced
to be conspiratorial find secret adherents inside the power-structures
that stand against them, whether they be Catholics or Protestants
under bigoted regimes, or fascists and communists under contrary dic-
tatorships.

If, as is probable, the support of these two unknown and otherwise

---

[1] John 19, 33–34.
[2] Adolf Harnack, the great biblical scholar, dated its composition to the 70s.
[3] Acts 13, 27–29: DS.
[4] Mark 14, 55 and 64.
[5] Joseph and Arimathea are not mentioned elsewhere. A tradition dating from the
thirteenth century identifies Arimathea with Ramleh, near Jaffa; but the town's foun-
dation most probably dates from the Omayyad caliphate. The legend that Joseph
brought the Grail to England has no valid historical support. John describes Nicodemus as the one who had previously visited Jesus by night.

silent persons has been retro-injected into the drama, Paul's fabric of events (minus the theology and the bias) is believable. Jesus had been put to death in a fashion that was calculated to diminish, if not destroy, spiritual power. But was this enough? Those executing controversial figures do what they can, when they have time to reflect, to prevent their victims achieving the status of martyrs. In 1916, for example, the British government reduced public sympathy for Sir Roger Casement by circulating a diary which discredited him as a man, not as an Irish nationalist. Often the preferred means are primitively physical. The Germans hanged after the Nuremberg Trials were burned (despite the fact that half of them belonged to a church which then condemned cremation) and their ashes dumped from a dustbin into the Rhine. It was logical for the enemies of Jesus to wish to obtain and dispose of his corpse. This posed no grave administrative problem. Romans instructed in Jewish folk-ways would understand a wish that the three bodies should not defile the Passover or prompt any activity to do with burial on the sabbath.

Paul's preservation of this earlier version is important for resolving a problem which must otherwise puzzle readers of the New Testament. The synoptics relate that the women who followed Jesus had observed his entombment and planned to carry out the appropriate funerary rites when the sabbath was over.[1] Yet John tells us that the two Sanhedrin members had already saturated the shrouded body with aromatic oils. He gives their quantity: the equivalent of seventy-five pounds, or almost twice the luggage allowance of an airline tourist.

If Matthew is right, and the high priests secured permission, on Saturday, to mount armed guards at the entrance to the tomb, it may have been to protect the unguents from theft.

The use of the new tomb, confirmed in all accounts, may have been inspired by motives far removed from those of honouring a martyred sage. It may have been seen as a place of temporary disposal; the corpse of a crucified heretic could defile an occupied tomb. The purpose of the unguents may have been to facilitate cremation on Saturday night, when the sabbath was over.

Cremation, the method used by Hindus, Greeks and Romans to dispose of their dead was, though abhorrent to the Hebrews, familiar to them. To the south-west of the temple the rocky earth formed a depression, known in Hebrew as Gehinnom, malodorous with the stench of burning bodies. Gehinnom, which gives Christendom its Gehenna and Islam its *jahannam*, first acquired its association with future torment from the past sacrifice of children. A reforming seventh-century king, after expelling prostitutes of both sexes from the temple, had 'desecrated the furnace in the Valley of Ben-Hinnom, so that no

[1] Luke 23, 55; Matthew 27, 61; Mark 15, 47.

one could make his son or daughter pass through fire in honour of Molech'.[1] But according to an indignant prophet, children were similarly sacrificed to Yahweh.[2] Under the Roman occupation the valley was used for burning municipal rubbish and the bodies of malefactors.

Let us suppose that on Saturday night (in the sabbath's wake) a secretive cortège took a roundabout route to this desolate valley, the crucified body slung across an ass. As the enemies of Jesus watched it burn, perhaps near the corpses of his two crucified companions, they will have felt assured that his legend would not again disturb their interests. A pile of ash provides no focus for popular devotion.

Scrutiny of police evidence cannot confirm this supposition, as no such evidence survives. Yet material that does survive hints that the body of Jesus did not lie on the tomb's cold slab until the intervention of a miracle stirred his shroud.

Credal formulae still regularly recited in myriad churches[3] declare that after his burial Jesus descended into hell, the English translation of the Greek´. If these embody a rumour that his body had been taken to the valley of burning, it was a rumour which neither his friends nor enemies would have wished to clarify: his friends lest it damage his awe, his enemies lest it damage their reputations. The idiosyncratic Paul, in his eulogy of charity, uses the phrase, 'If I give my body to be burned,' as an instance of the highest sacrifice. Paul, in general indifferent to the earthly life of Jesus, may here have referred to a circumstance which symbolised for him the necessary union of sacrifice with charity. Clement of Alexandria, whose intellect differs from that of most early Christians in its relaxed commingling of elements from Hellenistic and Semitic culture, who delighted in characterising Jesus as 'the Torchbearer' or 'the Hierophant', terms taken from the pagan mysteries, leaves a clearer hint. In a passage likening the body we wear in this life to our glorified future garment, he argues that the transition is achieved by fire. He abandons his doctrine of reserve to state boldly: 'Even Christ rose "through fire". Fire is here the agent, not of chastisement, but of that mysterious sublimation by which our organism is fitted for existence in a new sphere.'[4] Clement argues that the glorified body has the same relationship to our present body as the grain of corn to the new ear.

For if his enemies had hoped to burn Jesus from history, they were to find, too late, that cremation had an unforeseen disadvantage. When it began to be said that Jesus had risen from the dead, a convincing cadaver would have been the best refutation. But to claim that they

[1] Cf. II Kings 23 for the reforms of King Josiah, BC 637–608.
[2] Jeremiah 7, 31.
[3] Notably in the Apostles' Creed and the Creed of Athanasius.
[4] Paedagogus 1.VI. 46,3.

had burnt the body would have invited disbelief – and rumours that Jesus had indeed been seen began to spread within two days of his death.

On the morning after the sabbath, very early, Mary of Magdala went to the tomb. Evidently unaware that the body had already been anointed, she intended to begin the funerary rites. Even if, as some accounts suggest, she were accompanied by other women, she would hardly have carried anything approaching the weight of unguents lavished by Nicodemus. Once in the garden, she was alarmed to find that the entrance to the room-shaped recess was no longer protected from thieves and animals by its round stone door. She had come too late. On the slab within she could see only the linen shroud which had enfolded the naked body and the napkin which had covered the face. Mary ran to tell the disturbing news to Peter and John.

The gospels intrude stories of angelic presence into the Sunday dawn. Because of Peter's presence among the early witnesses (Paul, with significant misogyny, names him as the first, omitting Mary)[1] Mark's account is the most interesting as well as the simplest.

> On entering the tomb they (Mary and two female companions) saw a young man in a white robe seated on the right-hand side, and they were struck with amazement. But he said to them, 'There is no cause for alarm. You are looking for Jesus of Nazareth, who was crucified: he has risen, he is not here. See, here is the place where they laid him. But you must go and tell his disciples and Peter, "He is going before you to Galilee; it is there you will see him, just as he told you." '[2]

The empty tomb does not prove a miracle and was not thought to do so in early Christian times. The reappearances of Jesus, not the empty tomb, gave the thrust to belief and polemic. The emptiness proves only that the crucified body had left the tomb some time between the Friday afternoon, when the women had seen Jesus laid there, and the Sunday morning of Mary's visit. How the body came to be absent has been variously explained. The founders of Christian orthodoxy argued that, at a moment unknown, in an action unwitnessed, the divine power had raised Jesus's body to new life. This new life was conceived

[1] We may be sure, on the grounds of 'awkwardness', that the discoverers of the empty tomb were women. The evidence of women was devalued in Jewish society and the early church would have preferred the discoverers to have been men.

[2] Mark 16, 5–8: DS. Mark uses the same Greek diminutive – *neaniskos* – for the young man at the tomb as he used for the young man who escaped arrest by abandoning his shroud. On this occasion the young man wears a stole, a long white robe coming to the feet such as was worn by priests and patricians. It is tempting to see in the youth of Thursday a still earlier visitor to the Sunday tomb and the percipient of a yet earlier apparition.

in different ways. Paul saw it as being manifested in a spiritual body, which he carefully distinguishes from the body of everyday life. At the other extreme, Jesus was imagined to reinhabit the same body which had died on the cross. This second, materialistic view ignores the difficulty that on several important occasions Jesus was not to be immediately recognised by those to whom he appeared. Mary of Magdala, for example, mistook him for the gardener until he pronounced her name; Clopas and his companion on their way to Emmaus[1] recognised their fellow-wayfarer when he broke bread with them at supper.

The precise nature of the resurrection – or reappearance – of Jesus has been endlessly debated; in particular what kind of body Jesus used after death.

To gnostic groups and individuals the question was hardly important. Many held that Jesus had occupied, throughout his life, a body akin to a phantasm; what hung on the cross had been an appearance only. This view, named docetism from the Greek verb 'to seem', was held in various versions. In one, a substitute victim is crucified in place of Jesus: Judas was naturally a popular substitute.

The gnostic view of matter is not entirely remote from the picture provided by modern physics. The gnostics intuited that a living entity is akin to a flame that constantly changes. Traditional materialism's picture of a pattern of irreducible atoms moving like billiard balls on theoretically calculable paths no longer seems as 'scientific' as in the past. But on an important level the gnostic view conflicts with experience. For even if the solidity of matter is an ultimate illusion, it is an illusion to which we are subject. Common sense was thus one factor which led to the decline of docetism.[2]

The eighteenth century, in a characteristic reaction to the generations that had accepted a physical miracle, produced a new theory: Jesus had not really died on the cross but had fallen into a death-like coma from which he had been revived. An early proponent of this idea was Karl Friedrich Bahrdt (1741–1792), who believed that Joseph of

[1] The village of Imwas, or Emmaus, no longer exists. It was bulldozed for security reasons by the Israelis after their occupation of the West Bank in 1967; its site has since been covered by a featureless forest, 'Canada Park'. See Michael Adams, *Sunday Times*, June 1968.

[2] Another was the seventh-century rise of Islam, a new religion containing docetic elements. The Koran does not deny that Jesus was mortal, contrary to some docetist teaching. 'Peace is upon me,' Jesus says in Sura 19, vv. 34–35, 'the day of my birth and the day of my death, and the day of my being raised up alive.' It is disputed whether the latter refers to an individual resurrection, or the general resurrection. One of the most discussed passages in the Koran rebukes the Jews for saying, 'We killed the Messiah, Jesus, the son of Mary, the messenger of God' (Sura 4, vv. 154–159). The discussion here centres on whether it is the death on the cross that is denied, or the boast that men, not Providence, had contrived it. Cf. Geoffrey Parrinder: *Jesus in the Qur'an*, London, 1965.

Arimathea and Nicodemus were members of a secret Essene brother-hood which opposed the *naïf*, nationalist conception of the messiah. They trained Jesus to be a messiah of rationalism and prepared him to face the ordeal of apparent death. After removing his comatose body from the cross, Joseph of Arimathea used secret remedies which enabled him on the third day to leave the tomb. Karl Heinrich Venturini (1768–1849), who ascribed the healing miracles to a portable medicine chest, believed that Jesus survived death thanks to a superb constitution. The Germans' idea was to be taken up by a host of novelists. D. H. Lawrence's *The Man Who Died* had as its first title *The Escaped Cock – A Story of the Resurrection*: its theme, in Lawrence's words, that 'Jesus gets up and feels very sick about everything, and can't stand the old crowd any more – so cuts out'.[1] Robert Graves (with Joshua Podro) imagined, in *Jesus in Rome*, a revived Chrestus causing disturbances in the imperial capital.

But the evidence all indicates that Jesus did die, that the tomb was empty when Mary of Magdala visited it and that thereafter Jesus appeared to many. The assumption that Mark was right and all the Sanhedrin convicted him, and that Paul was rightly informed in his version of the burial, leaves the way open for an interpretation of Jesus's reappearance which does not depend on the supernatural re-vitalisation of a dead body. The cremation of his earthly remains makes it easier, not more difficult, to arrive at this interpretation.

The most likely explanation for the dramatic change in the disciples' morale lies in their conviction that Jesus had reappeared to individuals and to groups after his crucifixion. A contrary interpretation, that the disciples conspired to exploit a Jesus they knew to be dead and finished, would raise more problems than it could resolve. If the Galileans had been hardened criminals, and if the cause had offered immediate gain, things might have been other. But the disciples had shown themselves unhardened even against sleep; their defeated cause promised and, in the first two centuries produced, few material rewards. Only a certainty that Jesus was a living, powerful presence led the previously weak-kneed to lives of endeavour and martyrdom.

The reappearances are described in various episodes. His form was sometimes immediately recognisable, sometimes and more mysteriously it first assumed the lineaments of a gardener or wayfarer. Each report is open to doubt. Even orthodox scholars are wary of pinning their faith to the account of one single appearance or particular detail. For one thing, the concluding portions of Mark and John, the richest sources, are textually suspect. The greatest scepticism attaches not to the apparitions but to the sayings attributed to Jesus after death. No

[1] See Harry T. Moore: *The Intelligent Heart, The Story of D. H. Lawrence*, London, 1955: p. 364.

saying is intrinsically more convincing than Paul's aural experience on the road to Damascus: *Saul, Saul, why are you persecuting me?* In that case we can trace the utterance at least in part to Paul's unconscious. He had probably watched the stoning of Stephen and had certainly persecuted the followers of Jesus. The words he heard were an irruption of repressed material into a sensitive consciousness. Love, guilt, desire, may have prompted other utterances, just as the editorial process may have been at work on the form in which these have come down to us. But when all this is conceded, the fact that the disciples believed that Jesus had died but still in a real sense lived, is part, and an important part, of human history.

In an age which cannot accept the bursting tomb of Renaissance painting and yet finds the rationalism of the eighteenth century facile, how can we approach the resurrection?

India has opened one approach, modern England another. The reappearance of Indian holy men is an experience reported as frequently in the trousered present as the kilted past. For example, at 3 pm on 19 June 1936, in a bedroom at the Regent Hotel, Bombay, his guru seems to have appeared to a modern Yogi and discoursed with him for the space of two hours. Sri Yukteswar, the guru, had recently died and his disciple, the autobiographer Paramahansa Yogananda, had supervised his funeral. (Householders, Yogananda tells us, are commonly cremated but swamis and monks are thought to have already been cremated in the fire of wisdom at the taking of their vows. Yukteswar had been buried.) In a life of just over eighty years, the guru, like Jesus, had cured people of illness, specifically diabetes, tuberculosis and even cholera. Yogananda far exceeds the gospel-writers in the space he devotes to what his dead guru told him of this world and the next. The scepticism of biblical scholars over the precise content of the post-resurrectional utterances of Jesus is echoed when we read: 'Among the fallen dark angels, expelled from other worlds, friction and war take place with lifetronic bombs or mental mantric vibratory rays.' One asks whether the guru spoke in English – for there are echoes of the popular science of the day, to say nothing of Milton – or whether in the Bengali which the Nobel prize-winning Rabindranath Tagore had exploited for his high-flown, rather drawn-out poetry. But while one asks sceptical questions about the literal accuracy of the transcription of the guru's posthumous sermon, Yogananda's belief that he had seen his beloved master carries conviction. It is to be noted that the yogi takes the apparition as something benign and normal. He never feels fear.[1]

Since rationalism applied its knife to the mysterious, the nineteenth and twentieth centuries have seen a contrary swing, in some cases to

[1] See Paramahansa Yogananda: *Autobiography of a Yogi*, Los Angeles, 1975.

the occult, or more seriously to the scientific investigation of the para-normal. The Society for Psychical Research was founded in 1882, not by the type of person who turns to astrology or the Tarot, but by learned Oxford and Cambridge dons. In organising, as almost its first collective function, a census of hallucinations, the Society showed a willingness to take seriously the class of phenomenon in which his disciples' perception of Jesus after his death must surely stand. Over four hundred collectors posed the same question to some seventeen thousand people: 'Have you ever, when believing yourself to be completely awake, had a vivid impression of seeing or being touched by a living being or inanimate object, or of hearing a voice; which impression, so far as you could discover, was not due to any external physical cause?'

Nearly ten per cent of this sample group affirmed that they had undergone some such experience.

This census gave G. N. M. Tyrrell material for a classic discussion of the subject, *Apparitions*.[1] Tyrrell applied the sober, unemotional approach to his subject of one who had been trained as an electrical engineer. He classified four types of reported apparition: those resulting from conscious experimentation, when an agent tries to make his apparition visible to a particular percipient; those occurring in moments of crisis to the percipient; those appearing sufficiently long after the death of the person represented in the apparition for there to be no such coincidence with a crisis; apparitions which habitually haunt certain places as 'ghosts'. Some of the best attested apparitions are those of the living to the living. In one classic example, two Norfolk brothers had married two Norfolk sisters and the two households lived a mile and a quarter apart. A guest staying with brother A sees from the window a trap arriving with brother B seated beside his wife. They drive by without stopping but not before brother A has made some comment on the horse. But shortly afterwards the couple in fact turn up. They had thought of making the visit and then acted on the thought. Somehow brother B had projected an inner event into the minds of several people in the other household who had seen the intention as an apparition. Crisis apparitions were apparently common in the farflung Empire. British soldiers dying in India would appear at the moment of death to relations in England.

How does Tyrrell's theory of apparitions relate to the experience whose effect on the disciples altered history? Tyrrell presupposes that all perception involves an inner action. We habitually assume that we see objects as external realities; but in fact the pattern of colours and lines which perception involves is the result of sensory messages delivered to, and interpreted by, the receiver's mind. The messages are

[1] G. N. M. Tyrrell: *Apparitions*; with a preface by H. H. Price, Wykeham Professor of Logic in the University of Oxford, London, 1943.

sometimes misread, as when we mistake a tree for a man. Or sometimes, under the influence of drugs or alcohol, we perceive convincing
illusions, the true hallucination. But with the genuine apparition, as in
the experience of Mary of Magdala and the other disciples, the person
who appears, the agent, projects a sensory construct into the minds of
one or more percipients. Such apparitions are to be distinguished from
the stage ghost which writes letters or moves a dagger. The true apparition is an internal event in the mind of the percipient. It is distinguished from the pink elephant seen by the victim of alcoholic
excess in being pulsed out by an agent, another existing mind.

The assurance of hundreds of disciples[1] that they had seen Jesus
alive sustained a revolutionary decade. From the crucifixion to Paul's
first conference in Jerusalem with Peter and James[2] the followers of
Jesus – or Chrestus – were breaking the vessels of the past to make all
things new. An alternative kingdom exists here and now within the
brutal empire within all societies in all ages. It is open to Jews and gentiles, men and women, slaves and free. Possessions are shared, barriers
dissolved. It can be entered not by obedience to a system of laws or
emigration to a physical place. What is required is recognition of man's
true citizenship, or better, family. And the bond of this family is the
common meal. To it Jews and gentiles bring particular gifts. A very
early eucharistic rite is close to a sabbath celebration. The cup of wine
precedes the breaking of bread. There is no link with the cross, no
rehearsal of death. The bread is broken to simple words:

> We thank you, our father,
> For the life and the gnosis
> Which you have revealed to us through your servant Jesus.[3]

At the meal's conclusion the god of Jesus was thanked for living in
their hearts, 'as well as for the gnosis, faith and immortality you have
made known to us'. Greeks, finding a bedrock of certainty in their
speculative marsh, see in Jesus the torchbearer through the labyrinth
of this world's values. They treasure his assurance:

> In this world you will have anxiety; but take heart: I have defeated
> the world.[4]

Cosmos means more than world; it means the universe which can be

---

[1] Paul puts them at more than five hundred: 1 Corinthians 15, 6.
[2] The first 'bishop', Joseph's eldest son, who in his personal life never abandoned the
practice of Judaism.
[3] The *Didache*, or Teaching of the Twelve Apostles, dates from the end of the first
century or the beginning of the second. See Johannes Weiss: *Earliest Christianity; A
History of the Period AD 30–150*, New York, 1959: pp. 62–63.
[4] John 16, 33: DS.

apprehended by the senses, the level of reality subject to evil stars and malicious despots.

But even before this creative decade was half over, the tendency to jealous faction had shown itself in the squabbles over widows' rations. The abandonment of rules alarmed the leaders and what happens to most prophets happened to Jesus: out of reverent but prudent love his followers stood him on his head. The anti-nomian opponent of the temple was to be reclaimed for sacrifice. The gospels intended to announce his good news present him as endorsing the same legal system he had been convicted of defying. After the Romans destroyed the temple in AD 70, 'Christians', those claiming that Jesus had been the messiah, fashioned a new ecclesiastical structure which, they claimed, replaced but continued the old. A hierarchy of deacons, priests and bishops – all, except in the church of Marcion, male – presented the packaged instructions which human beings generally prefer to the responsibilities of freedom.

But while a fictitious Christ became the ikon of a persecuting cult and his cross the talisman of Byzantine arms, the man who had risen through fire cannot be suppressed. Edited gospels, intricate doctrines, permit, like the olive boles in the Bethany garden, glimpses of the incendiary who had challenged death. If all the things he had done were written down, the fourth gospel concludes, the world itself could not store the books so written. As history proceeds down its highway of crime, Jesus points upward to a knowledge which frees the self. In the darkest night he is hidden, not extinguished. To each generation he speaks in glittering fragments. Every morning, like Hêlios, he is born again.

The Four Canonical Gospels As Sources For Biography

The four documents which introduce the New Testament were written, most critical opinion agrees, in Greek during the last third of the first century or, in the case of John, a few years later. Early in the literary history of Christianity we detect two different ways of approaching the gospels: harmonisation on the one hand; analysis on the other.

The way of harmonisation is based on the assumption that every single sentence, episode, saying, sermon and prayer is literally and historically true. And that, therefore, if only the right formula could be hit on, all four narratives could be dovetailed together to produce a perfect biography of Jesus, in which every obscurity, every apparent contradiction, would disappear, having been resolved.

From Tatian in the sub-Apostolic age to Archbishop Goodier in our own, this approach has appealed to those who cling to the theological notion of the literal inspiration of scripture, with human agency reduced merely to the hand that held the pen; as also to all who believe that everything recorded about Jesus is precious. So it is. But this method does not produce the results intended.

The way of analysis has a no less ancient pedigree. Papias, whose works are, alas, only preserved to us in quotation, showed the greatest curiosity about the authors of the gospels, what race (hence what culture) they belonged to, what sources they drew on for their *differing* treatment of their subject.

Following this line of thought, Christian historians over the centuries have affirmed that Mark had access to the memories of Peter, or that Matthew was a Jew writing for Jewish converts, or that Luke was a Greek writing for Greeks who may even have had access to Jesus's mother as source for his detailed treatment of the Saviour's birth and childhood. Grains of truth, and grains of fantasy, nonetheless reflecting an inquisitive approach to scripture entirely compatible with our own twentieth century attitude of mind.

Once it is seen, as Papias (c. AD 130) never seems to have doubted,

that the authors of the gospels wrote as human authors and not as auto-
mata, that they were not only conditioned in their points of view by the
culture to which they belonged but also exercised freedom of choice
over what they put in and what they left out, and that the work of each
was directed to a different readership, the relevance of harmonising
their differing statements disappears, or if not its relevance, then certainly its urgency.

Thus, the Gospel of Mark appears to have been addressed to gentile
Christians who did not understand the Aramaic phrases still evidently
part of the living tradition relating to Jesus, and which the author is at
pains to explain; who were also unfamiliar with the Old Testament, to
which he rarely refers; but were familiar with Latin terms concerning
matters military, legal and fiscal, which he uses more liberally than the
other evangelists. His is a dynamic but doomed Christ surrounded by
doltish disciples.

The Gospel of Matthew, by contrast, seems to have been composed
by a Jewish Christian aware of the doubts harboured by his Jewish
Christian proselytes. While drawing heavily on Mark for his narrative,
the writer inflates his borrowed material with an immense number of
often inaccurate or inappropriate quotations from the Old Testament,
persuasive, we may suppose, to people who found the Marcan version
of the Good News – in its devastating simplicity – unconvincing unless
buttressed up and, as it were, authenticated by tags from the canonical
writers of the religion into which they had been born and which they
were nervously forsaking. His Christ is a menacing judge with hieratic
disciples to attend him.

Luke, also borrowing heavily from Mark but conveying the same
Good News to Greek readers with cultivated literary tastes, emphasises
that the message is for women as well as men, selects episodes and
characters for their typicality, is master equally of the pathetic and the
marvellous, telling his story in the back-projected light of the Passion
and Resurrection in such a way as to lure his readers into belief. His
Christ is a suave culture-hero who at the last rises physically into the
heavens.

John, with an even more obviously theological aim, writes of Jesus
from the outset as an emanation of the Creator. The Creator's creative
Word made flesh, he is temporarily a man, but permanently God. And
that is the message, illustrated by lofty discourses and very mysterious
godlike actions.

We see then that the purpose of each writer was different, whatever
the individual reason may have been. The organisation and selection of
the material is different, since designed to produce a different effect.
And since each evangelist wrote only to instruct, this necessarily
implies an organising theory imposed on the original facts, whatever

they were or were thought to have been at a considerable remove from the date of their occurrence.

The very word evangelist means the bearer of a theological message. He is not the same as the historian. And the historian *behind* the evangelists is the very person we lack, who might have told us what the real facts were on which the evangelists produced their theological constructs.

That the theology of the Early Church developed at very high speed can be seen by comparing the naturalistic Christ of Mark with the Incarnate God of John, which cannot be separated by more than forty years at the most. The development reaches a point where the cynical might be tempted to think that theology can manufacture historical facts as it grows. And this is indeed the case.

To take one isolated example of how theology can alter historical fact – the 'awkward', i.e. unassimilable, scraps of information preserved in the gospels point to a summer crucifixion (see my chapter XVI). Matthew and John, alike reflecting preoccupations of the Early Church, would have it coincide with the Jewish Passover, though they disagree over which precise day of the festival. Let us opt for an early dating of Matthew and a late dating of John, and conclude that this was the approved theological construct for the second half of the first Christian century. Yet, a century later, Tertullian (AD 153–220 approx.) – to be followed by that commanding theologian Augustine of Hippo (AD 354–430) – was categoric that the crucifixion had occurred on 25 March, quite near Passover indeed, but actually coinciding with the Christian feast of the Annunciation, 'for it was fitting that....' Well, yes, we don't need to be told that this marian feast had become well-entrenched in the Christian calendar by this time and that, as Christ's human life had begun in the Virgin's womb on 25 March, so it was fitting that it should end on the cross on 25 March some thirty-three years later (nearer forty in all likelihood), thus presenting X-number of perfect years of an earthly existence perfect in all other respects hitherto save those mathematical and calendrical.

This shows how theological constructs grow, and when the evangelists were putting pen to papyrus less than a hundred years before Tertullian's birth, the process was already far advanced.

Hence it becomes of the greatest importance to probe behind the didactic theological constructs in any quest for the historical personality and facts of Jesus – the Foreigner. Only then can any valid harmonisation begin.

APPENDIX B

The Crucifixion and the Passover

The notion that Jesus was crucified at Passover has passed into the assumptions of Christendom. Because of the ineluctable movement to link him with Old Testament patterns and prophecies, Jesus is equated with the sacrificial lamb. Professor Raymond E. Brown posits 'five stages in the composition of John, with each step representing a step further away from the primitive tradition'. The editors who worked on John in ancient times allowed, or overlooked, one significant breach with the synoptic pattern. The author of the fourth gospel states categorically that the last supper took place *before* Passover. If, as seems to this author probable, John had really shifted the crucifixion to a day many months *before* Passover – to the previous August – this fact has been smothered.

If the synoptics were correct in their dating, and the last supper was a Passover meal, we could make certain confident assumptions. The Torah preserves precise instructions from Yahweh to Moses and Aaron governing the manner in which the Hebrews were to commemorate their delivery from Egypt. At sunset on the fourteenth day of the first month (this means Nisan, the first month of the religious year which fell in the spring) a male lamb or kid was to be slaughtered by each family or group. The animal so sacrificed had to be in its first year and to be without blemish:

> And they shall take the blood, and strike it on the two side posts and on the upper door post of the houses, wherein they shall eat it. And they shall eat the flesh in that night, roast with fire, and unleavened bread; and with bitter herbs they shall eat it. Eat not of it raw, nor sodden at all with water, but roast with fire; his head with his legs, and with the purtenance thereof. And ye shall let nothing of it remain until the morning; and that which remaineth of it until the morning ye shall burn with fire.

Yahweh had defined the spirit in which the meal should be eaten:

> And thus shall ye eat it; with your loins girded, your shoes on your feet, and your staff in your hand; and ye shall eat it in haste; it is the Lord's passover.

Moses himself told the Hebrews:

> and none of you shall go out at the door of his house until the morning.[1]

It is to be noted that the synoptics describe none of the rituals mentioned. At the conclusion of the meal all the diners go out of the house and walk to the Mount of Olives. The synoptics also picture a Jerusalem in which masses of other informed people are defying the Passover rules: from the High Priests conspiring to investigate Jesus to the temple guards who are being prepared to arrest him in collusion with a detachment of Roman soldiers.

John not only changes the dating – 'it was just before the Passover feast' – but has Jesus institute the sacrament of bread and wine, much earlier, in a synagogue at Capernaum (John 6,59) and not at the last supper.

---

[1] Exodus 12 preserves the most detailed account. Verse 22 contains the ordinance against leaving the house during the night of commemoration.

Elias – or Hêlios?

Both Mark and Matthew report, in Greek letters, what they think to have been the sentence in the language Jesus used. The first two words in Mark are *elôi elôi* (ἐλωι ἐλωι) while Matthew has *êli êli* (ἠλι ἠλι). The typological linking of the Twenty-Second Psalm to the circumstances of Jesus's death is common to all four gospels as they now stand. The psalmist complains that 'they part my garments among them, and cast lots upon my vesture'. All three synoptics say this is what happened in the case of Jesus. The psalmist's lament – 'They pierced my hands and feet' – suggests the use of nails, which is confirmed in accounts of Jesus's reappearance after death. In fact, nails were unlikely to have been used to support the weight of a body in a punishment whose anguish was compounded by its long duration.

If Jesus had meant 'my god', the usual form would have been *ilahi*, as the *Jerusalem Bible* notes. If the *elôi* and *êli* of the gospel tradition mask an original *Êlie*, C. H. Turner's words are worth quoting: '... what more likely than that non-Jewish Orientals, to many of whom *El* or *Eli* (*Heli*) was the name of their sun-god, hearing the cry and connecting it with the reappearance of the sun, should suppose that Jesus had called on the sun and been answered by it, and that they, or one of them, should have gone on to say, "Let us see whether after all Helios is coming to take him down"?'[1] Such a bystander may have heard the vocative correctly, but not understood the irony behind it.

As for the use of macaronic, Geza Vermes quotes the Palestinian Targum (Pseudo-Jonathan) to Numbers 11, 26 for rendering in an extraordinary Greco-Aramaic glossalalia the prophetic message of the two elders, colleagues of Moses, who were seized by the Holy Spirit: 'The lord (*Kiris*) is present (*etimos hetoimos*) to them in the moment of distress (*aniki ananke*).' Vermes comments (as we have quoted earlier in the text): 'a mixture of Aramaic and Greek would have been more or less intelligible to most Jews in the first century AD.'[2]

As late as Constantinian times, the cult of Hêlios was still so wide-

[1] C. H. Turner: *A New Commentary on Holy Scripture*, London, 1928: New Testament section, p. 118.
[2] Op. cit., p. 113.

spread in Syria that Christian preachers were only able to suppress it by substituting for him the prophet Elias. The confusion between the two names was as long lasting as the confusion over P and B in popular Arabic.

Select Bibliography

ALAND, K. *Synopsis Quattuor Evangeliorum* (Stuttgart, 9th ed., 1976).
    Antipater of Thessalonica. Cf. *The Garland of Philip* (ed. A. S. F. Gow & D. L. Page, Cambridge, 1968).
APULEIUS. *The Golden Ass* (tr. Robert Graves, London, 1950).
BELLINZONI, A. J. *The Sayings of Jesus in the Writings of Justin Martyr* (Leiden, 1967).
BELL, H. I. *Egypt From Alexander the Great to the Arab Conquest* (Oxford, 1948).
BELL, H. I. *Cults and Creeds in Graeco-Roman Egypt* (Liverpool, 1953).
BIGG, C. *The Christian Platonists of Alexandria*; Bampton Lectures for 1886 (Oxford, 1913).
BLACKMAN, E. C. *Marcion And His Influence* (London, 1948).
BRANDON, S. G. F. *The Trial of Jesus of Nazareth* (London, 1968).
BREASTED, J. H. *Development of Religion and Thought in Ancient Egypt* (New York, 1912).
BROWN, R. E. *The Gospel According to John* (2 vols., New York, 1966).
BUDGE, E. A. W. *The Egyptian Book of The Dead* (New York, 1967).
BULTMANN, R. *Primitive Christianity in its Contemporary Setting* (tr. R. H. Fuller, London, 1960).
BULTMANN, R. *The Studies of the Synoptic Gospels* in *Form Criticism, Two Essays on New Testament Research* (New York, 1962).
CAMPBELL THOMPSON, R. *Semitic Magic, Its Origins and Development* (London, 1908).
DERRETT, J. D. M. *Law in the New Testament* (London, 1970).
DODDS, E. R. *The Greeks and the Irrational* (Los Angeles, 1959).
DORESSE, J. *The Secret Books of the Egyptian Gnostics* (New York, 1960).
ENDO, S. A. *Life of Jesus* (tr. R. A. Schuchert, Tokyo, 1978).
FAHD, T. *La Divination Arabe – Études Religieuses, Sociologiques et Folkloriques sur le Milieu Natif de l'Islam* (Leiden, 1961).
FINEGAN, J. *The Archaeology of the New Testament* (Princeton, 1969).
GRANT, M. *Jesus* (London, 1977).
GRAVES, R. & PEDRO, J. *Jesus in Rome, An Historical Conjecture* (London, 1957).
GUIGNEBERT, C. *The Jewish World in the Times of Jesus* (New York, 1939).
HARRISON, R. K. *The Dead Sea Scrolls: An Introduction* (New York, 1961).
HICK, J. (ed.). *The Myth of God Incarnate* (London, 1977).
HOSKYNS, SIR E. & DAVEY, N. *The Riddle of the New Testament* (London, 1931).
JAMES, M. R. *The Apocryphal New Testament* (Oxford, 1924).
JAMES, W. *The Varieties of Religious Experience, A Study in Human Nature*; Gifford Lectures, Edinburgh 1901–2.
JEREMIAS, J. *Unknown Sayings of Jesus* (London, 1964).
JONAS, H. *The Gnostic Religion, The Message of the Alien God and the Beginnings of Christianity* (Boston, 1963).
KAHLE, P. E. *The Cairo Geniza* (Oxford, 1959).

KLAUSNER, J. *Jesus of Nazareth, His Life, Times and Teaching* (London, 1925).

LACARRIÈRE, J. *The Gnostics;* preface by Lawrence Durrell (tr. N. Rootes, London, 1977).

MACCOBY, H. *Revolution in Judaea – Jesus and the Jewish Resistance* (London, 1973).

MAYASSIS, S. *Mystères et Initiations de l'Égypte Ancienne* (Athens, 1957).

MEAD, G. R. S. *Fragments of A Faith Forgotten* (London, 1900).

MEINARDUS, O. F. A. *Christian Egypt, Ancient and Modern* (Cairo, 1965).

MCARTHUR, H. K. *In Search of the Historical Jesus* (London, 1970).

NOCK, A. D. *Early Gentile Christianity and its Hellenistic Background* (New York, 1928).

PARRINDER, G. *Jesus in the Qur'an* (London, 1965).

PHILO OF ALEXANDRIA. *De Vita Contemplativa* (introduction & notes by F. Daumas, tr. into French by P. Miquel, Paris, 1963).

PLINY THE YOUNGER. *The Letters* (tr. B. Radice, London, 1963).

PUECH, H.-C. *Gnosis and Time, Man and Time*; papers for the Eranos notebooks (London, 1958).

ROBINSON, J. M. *The Nag Hamadi Library* (New York, 1977).

SCHURER, E. *A History of the Jewish People in the Time of Jesus* (Edinburgh, 1886–90).

SCHWEITZER, A. *The Quest of the Historical Jesus – A Critical Study of its Progress from Reimarus to Wrede* (first pub. 1906; London, 1963).

SMITH, M. *The Secret Gospel* (New York, 1973).

SMITH, M. *Jesus The Magician* (New York, 1978).

SPRATT, P. *Hindu Culture and Personality – A Psycho-Analytic Study* (Bombay, 1966).

SYME, R. *Tacitus* (2 vols., Oxford, 1958).

TACITUS. *Annalium Libri* (ed. C. D. Fisher, Oxford, 1958).

Thomas. The Gospel According to Thomas (Coptic text established and translated by A. Guillaumont, H.-C. Puech, G. Quispel and Yassah 'Abd al Masih, Leiden, 1976).

TYRRELL, G. N. M. *Apparitions* (London, 1943).

VERMES, G. *Jesus the Jew* (London, 1973).

WEISS, J. *Earliest Christianity – A History of the Period AD 30–150* (New York, 1959).

WILSON, R. McL. *The Gnostic Problem – A Study of the Relations between Hellenistic Judaism and the Gnostic Heresy* (London, 1958).

YOGANANDA, P. *Autobiography of a Yogi* (Los Angeles, 1975).

Index

Oxford University 2, 69, 157

Paedagogus (Clement of Alexandria) 152
Palestine 14, 19–20, 22, 26, 33–4, 37, 42,
    45, 61, 82, 85, 89, 91, 93, 98–9, 109,
    112, 117, 123–4, 131, 134, 137, 143
Palestinian Targum, The 166
Pallas Athene (Greek deity) 38
Pamukkale, Turkey 69
Pantera, Tiberius Julius Abdes 17–18
Papias (Christian historian) 69, 71, 88,
    161
Parables of Christ 33–34, 49–55, 62, 108,
    112; concerning money 34; Dives &
    Lazarus 108, 112; good Samaritan 50;
    house on rock/sand 33; importunate
    friend 34; lamp under tub 33; lost
    coin 34, 145; lost sheep 34; pearl of
    great price 34, 52, 135; pounds (talents)
    34, 50–2; prodigal son 52–5; sower 34;
    unjust steward 50–51; wicked vine-
    dressers 50–51
Parousia 73
Parrinder, Geoffrey 154
Parthenogenesis 15
Paschal lamb 73, 164
Passover, Feast of 5, 44, 62, 73, 82, 88,
    100, 113–4, 151, 163–5
Patmos, Island of 75
Patron (Egyptian police chief) 38
Paul of Tarsus 21, 29–30, 74–6, 126,
    150–6, 158; his letters 88–9, 134
Pearl, Hymn of the 54–5, 61, 87, 132, 139
Pelusium, Egypt 20
Pericles (Athenian statesman) 37
Persephone (Greek deity) 100, 133–4
Persia, Persian era, Persians 35, 37, 40,
    42, 44–5, 65
Peter (apostle) 21, 69, 80, 83, 107, 132,
    138, 144, 153, 158; as source for Mark
    58, 60, 62–3, 68, 72, 80–1, 85, 88, 110,
    125, 161; call of 4, 66–7; hails Jesus as
    messiah 72, 118; denies him 85, 111,
    131
Phaedo (friend of Socrates) 70
Pharisees 27–8, 46, 75, 78, 91, 93–5, 119,
    136–7
Pharos (*see* Alexandria)
Philip (apostle) 67–9, 81–2, 89, 106, 119
Philip, King of Macedon 141
Philip of Side 71
Philo of Alexandria 24, 46–7, 69, 88, 127;

his father 24; his nephew 24–5
Philostratus 96
Physiologus, (medieval bestiary) 15, 22
Phoenicia, Phoenicians 17, 124
Phoenix 22
Pilate, Pontius 43, 102–3, 126–9, 136–42,
    150
Pillars of Hercules 141
Piloti, Emmanuel (Venetian merchant)
    21
Plato, Platonists 15, 37, 39, 46, 87, 128,
    141, 149
Pliny the Elder 22
Pliny the Younger 137
Podro, Joshua 155
Porphyry (Alexandrian philosopher) 48
Porphyry, Bishop of Gaza 134
Poseidon (Greek deity) 24
Potamos, 33
Primitive Church 89–90, 149, 153, 158–
    9, 163
Prochorus 75
Procla (wife of Pilate) 127–9, 139–40, 142
Proserpine (*see* Persephone)
Psalms, Book of 45, 146, 166
Pseudo-Jonathan (*see Palestinian Targum*)
Ptah (Egyptian deity) 40
Ptolemaic dynasty 18–20, 24–5, 37–8, 41,
    61
Ptolemy III, King of Egypt 22, 38
Pumpkinification of Claudius, The
    (Seneca) 141
Punjab 35
Purim, Feast of 44
Pusey House, Oxford 2

Q, Quelle, gospel chapbook 86
Quest for the Historical Jesus, The (A.
    Schweitzer) 73
Quirinius, Governor of Syria 12, 14
Qumran, Palestine 73

Rachel (wife of Jacob) 52
Rafah, Palestine 20
Rakotis (quarter of Alexandria) 24
Ramleh, Palestine, 150
Rê (Egyptian sun-god) 17, 25, 40, 61, 134
    (*see also* Hêlios)
Redating the New Testament (J.A.T.
    Robinson) 70–1
Red Sea 35, 64